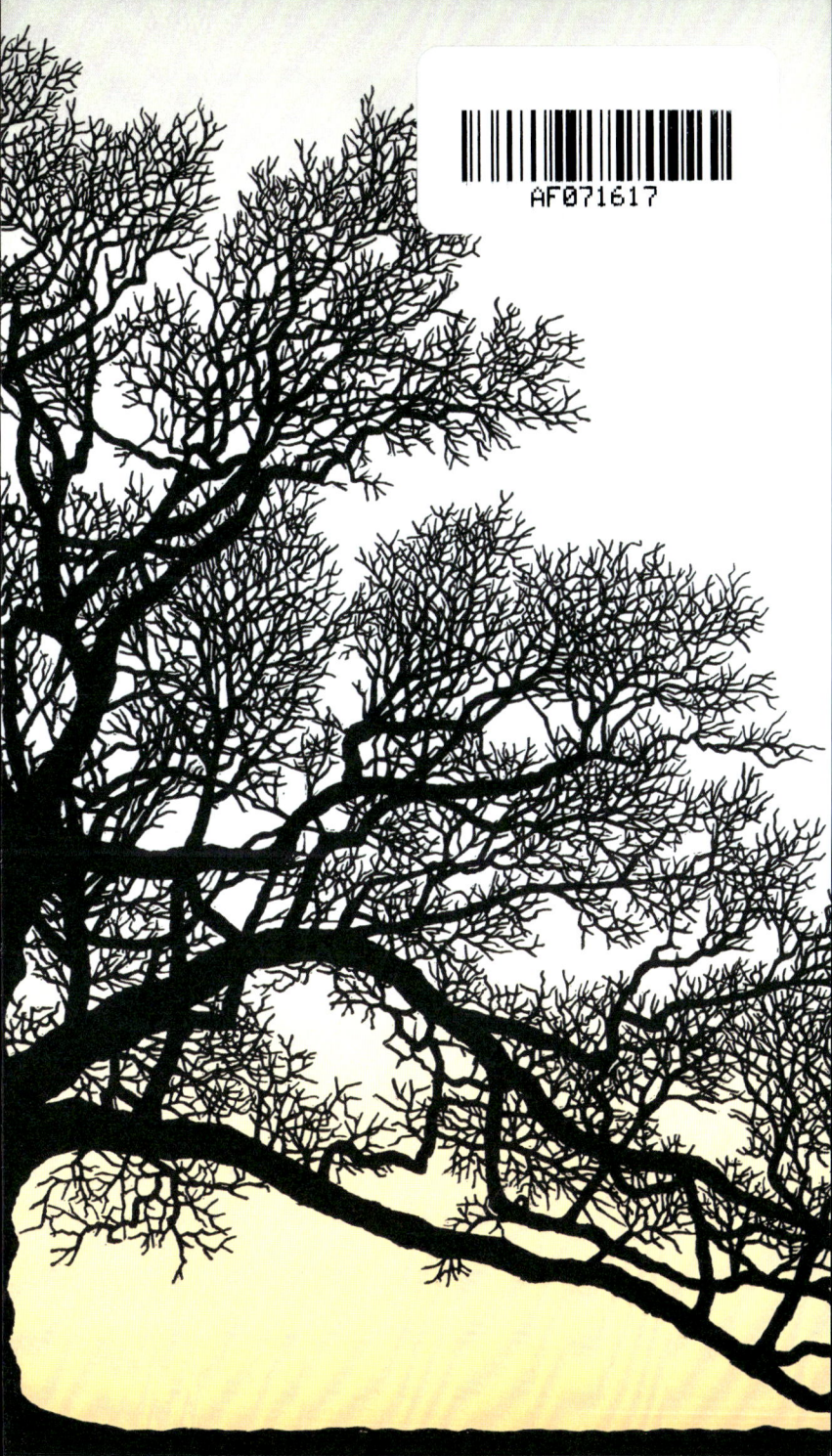

Trees in Winter

Trees in Winter

RICHARD SHIMELL

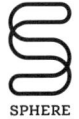

SPHERE

SPHERE

First published in Great Britain in 2024 by Sphere
This edition published in 2025 by Sphere

3 5 7 9 10 8 6 4 2

Copyright © Richard Shimell 2024

The moral right of the author has been asserted.

All rights reserved.
No part of this publication may be reproduced, stored in a
retrieval system, or transmitted, in any form or by any means, without
the prior permission in writing of the publisher, nor be otherwise circulated
in any form of binding or cover other than that in which it is published
and without a similar condition including this condition being
imposed on the subsequent purchaser.

A CIP catalogue record for this book
is available from the British Library.

ISBN 978-1-4087-3241-0

Typeset in Spectral by M Rules
Printed and bound in Great Britain by
Clays Ltd, Elcograf S.p.A

Papers used by Sphere are from well-managed forests
and other responsible sources.

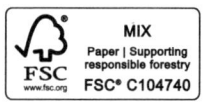

Sphere
An imprint of
Little, Brown Book Group
Carmelite House
50 Victoria Embankment
London EC4Y 0DZ

The authorised representative
in the EEA is
Hachette Ireland
8 Castlecourt Centre
Dublin 15, D15 XTP3, Ireland
(email: info@hbgi.ie)

An Hachette UK Company
www.hachette.co.uk

www.littlebrown.co.uk

For Pat Shimell and Andrew North

Contents

	Introduction	1
1	Wildness	7
2	Walking	25
3	Cornwall	43
4	Love and Printmaking	53
5	Rain	63
6	Printing Trees	77
7	Belonging	88
8	Boro Wood	98
9	Snow and Fog	109
10	Almost Wales	119

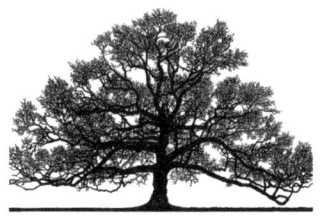

Introduction

If anyone had suggested I would enter my fifties as a professional printmaker making a living from carving intricate trees, inking and printing them and selling the results, I would have laughed. On the surface, there didn't seem to be anything in my life which pointed in that direction. I had no art education and no track record of drawing or painting as a hobby or otherwise. At school I gave up art in favour of history.

'Richard,' as my father often said, 'is no good with his hands.' I'm not sure what that judgement was based on. Perhaps it was my lack of interest in helping him fix things on his boat for long, cold and drizzly hours after school, when I would rather have been watching children's television – but it was damning in a family where the ability to make and repair was highly valued, and where I was so obviously failing to become the son my father wanted. I suspect it was also one of the reasons I took to printmaking so quickly after discovering it in my forties. It fulfilled a personal need. Not only was it a way into art – which I regretted having abandoned at school – it was also a means of proving him wrong. It turned out to be the path to an entirely new career.

Making art was deeply satisfying. It brought together the things I loved most. As a child I found escape in the woods and on the hills. As a troubled twenty-something, walking in the countryside saved me during difficult times. It ended up altering the direction of my life, eventually leading me out of London. When I found printmaking, my passion for walking suddenly had another purpose. The trees and landscapes I loved became more fascinating as I examined them differently, deconstructing and simplifying them as I wondered how I could turn them into prints. My relationship with what I saw deepened. As I walked, I watched out for the moments of beauty, and I tried to hold them in my head as I worked on my prints.

As a craft, printmaking is heavy on practical skills. Just as my cabinet-maker ancestors might have carved decorative finishes on furniture, I learned how to use tools to carve around the branches of a tree I had drawn on a solid block, removing the background to leave it in relief. I pushed this method to its extremes, exploring how detailed I could get, how fine a line I could leave raised on the surface and still ink and print it successfully.

I was lucky as a novice printmaker to find a style and subject early on which engaged me and was popular enough to allow me to make my living from it. People who like my prints sometimes tell me they now see and appreciate trees silhouetted against the light more often than they used to, and think of me when they do. I think that is the highest compliment.

Before printmaking, I worked as a freelance journalist and researcher, following twelve years' employment on local papers.

Introduction

I walked a lot and loved taking photos of landscapes and trees. I took hundreds, gaining an appreciation for composition, colour and a dramatic sky. I was tuned in to the drama of light, especially on those winter days when the low sun makes everything glow and the sky is dark from the passing rain or the shower to come. Every walk had its moments: the shape of a hill, the colour of the sky, the outline of a tree. I never knew what visual treasures I'd find.

I've always liked walking in winter, when the weather can be more dramatic, and the temperatures are lower, saving me from overheating or having to carry litres of water (which I'd need on a hot summer's day). It is also a time when the beautiful light and shadows of the golden hours just after dawn and before sunset are more accessible. I love walking in spring, summer and autumn too, but I think many of us overlook the beauty of winter, assuming it isn't a season in which to enjoy the outdoors. I don't necessarily prefer winter to the other three seasons, but there is so much to like about it, not least the bare and beautiful framework of a winter tree silhouetted against a bright sky.

Summer often disappoints. It seems impossible to imagine that it won't be warm and sunny, but so often it is not. As I started writing this book in August, it was so chilly I spent several afternoons wrapped in a blanket.

In winter our expectations are low enough to let us simply enjoy the unexpected bonus of a sunny day in December, or an unexpectedly warm one in February. Nobody remembers an averagely warm day in July, but I will never forget one February in Cornwall when it was warm enough to eat lunch in the garden, or that same month this year, when my temperature monitor registered 17°C in the shade and I sat indoors planning a walk, with the doors open and the birds singing. I will also never forget walks in the rain or in sub-zero temperatures, snug in my waterproofs, alone in the woods or on the moors, just enjoying the power of the weather or the emptiness. There isn't anything we can do to stop winter (apart from moving somewhere warmer), so we might as well look for the positives in it.

Of course, climate change might bring the south further north, but it's unlikely to make our winters dry and sunny. I remember attending a conference about climate change in Cornwall in the mid-1990s, where we were warned that wetter winters and warmer, drier summers would be the outcome for the county. That prediction is coming true. If only those in power had paid more attention then.

We are taught to dislike winter weather. The rain, the cold and the fog are loaded with negative associations: understandable if your job is outside, but of less importance if it is not. Many of us allow this cultural training to blind us to the beauty of a winter storm, the sight of rain blowing across a hillside or a woodland softened by mist. Children who happily play in puddles in the rain seem to turn into adults disinclined to venture out when the weather is wet. But, when you do, the rain is always less heavy, and the light is always brighter, than it looks from indoors.

I have always been fascinated by the weather and the natural world. I was lucky enough to grow up with easy access to beautiful countryside. As a child I would come home from school, collect the dog, hop over the fence and wander the fields and woods, building dams in the stream and keeping a log of the different birds I saw. I created ponds in the stream running through the garden by piling up walls of rock, then watched the rising water fill the natural hollows, changing it from one state into another. I'd let it reach the top of the dam, then push the wall over and watch the water gush out and a mini tidal wave set off downstream as I ran alongside. I loved the seasons and the way the stream filled up with plants in spring, until you could see no water, just green and later, flowers. It made me sad that my parents hacked it all down most years and mowed the small field next to it so often it became a drab lawn, when it could have been a flower-rich meadow.

In many ways I had a wonderful childhood. I didn't lack anything material. There was good food and a comfortable house. There was a downside, however. My parents' relationship was a difficult one and my father was an occasionally violent alcoholic. This was a subject no one was allowed to discuss unless you were looking for trouble. The silence around this problem created a strange dissonance. The family which appeared to have everything necessary for happiness was, in reality, one in which life was often difficult and awful things could happen. Love and honesty were hard to find.

Outside the home I had friends and fun, but when young I was sometimes bullied. My parents' reaction when I told them was simply, 'You need to stand up for yourself.' The problem was, they didn't explain how.

By my teens I was desperate to escape my family, but when I did, I was disappointed. I thought I would meet people like me at university, but I didn't. I was a lost young man, coming out in the era of AIDS, scared and unsure how to be gay, painfully self-conscious and lacking the skills to make friends or relationships.

I had no idea what I wanted to do in my life. I had no plan or direction, which wasn't helped by a feeling of antipathy towards the world of business and even the idea of having a career. I didn't get much guidance and neither I, nor my family, had connections of the kind which might have given me a foothold in a suitable profession.

I made bad decisions. I ended up in jobs I mostly disliked and which paid poor wages. My solace was walking, reading and the natural world, but that was tinged with sadness over the degradation of the countryside through modern farming methods. I sometimes felt I was walking in a world of loss: lost hedgerows, ploughed-up meadows, native woodland replaced by conifer plantations, over-grazed moorland, silent fields where lapwings used to flock in winter, and the vanished common land, often surviving only as a name on a map. I found hope in the un-farmed, or less intensively managed, land: the surviving commons and heaths, the little strips of wildness alongside coastal paths, the flower-rich downland hills too steep to plough, the old woods, the hedgerow trees and the roadside verges.

Eventually I managed to turn my life around. I escaped the city, where I had never belonged, and found a job I enjoyed for a while. Most importantly, with the help of a loving partner, I had choices, and could start to explore the things in which I was really interested. This allowed me to develop my creative side and led me to printmaking, which has profoundly changed my life.

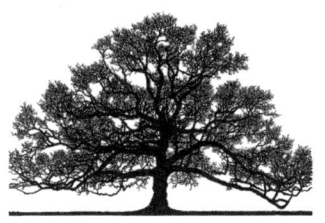

Wildness

Not long after I moved to south Devon, a spark of adventure and an urge to explore my new surroundings prompted me to put on my waterproofs and set out to trespass.

It was raining so heavily the water was pouring off the slopes and the road behind the house was running like a stream, so much so there were peaks and troughs in it, like miniature rapids. The trees at the top of the wooded hill opposite were hidden in mist.

The river, which flows through the valley below the house, rises in a marshy area of southern Dartmoor called Halshanger Common, about a mile up the hill and a 700-foot climb away. On a whim, I decided I wanted to follow the river to its source that day. The only way to do that was to walk on land where I had no right to be.

In truth, I had become addicted to walking, both to the endorphin rush from exercise and to the feeling of freedom and escape it gave me to be moving through the landscape. It had taken more than a year to sell our previous house, and free ourselves from a living situation which had become difficult. I had reached such levels of frustration and anxiety, I found it hard to concentrate at home. At that time, we lived on a hill in a village called Lapford, about 15 miles as the crow flies, or a half-hour drive, from the northern edge of Dartmoor. We had amazing views of the whole span of that part of the moor, including the highest peaks, Yes Tor and High Willhays. Whenever my work as a freelance journalist and editor allowed, I thought nothing of walking eight miles in an afternoon, then doing the same the next day. I walked so much I started losing weight and wondered if I had something wrong with me. Eventually I realised it was just the exercise.

In those days, before I moved south, the northern slopes of Dartmoor were the nearest piece of 'wild' landscape to me. I took myself off to the moor, anywhere from Sourton in the west to Drewsteignton in the east, but mostly to Belstone Common, Taw Marsh, Cosdon Hill or Belstone Cleave. These areas are mostly access land, so you can walk anywhere, provided you pay attention to flags signalling firing on the army training areas. It wasn't really wild, as it was grazed so heavily by livestock that much of it resembled a lawn, but it wasn't ploughed and mostly not fenced, and some of it was pleasingly scraggy with gorse, hawthorn and bracken. It was very different from the land which surrounded Lapford, where footpaths were routinely ploughed and planted over or obstructed by fences, including electric ones. I had tried all the footpath walks in the area, but had become tired of how complicated it was to get from one point to another – and bored of looking at farmland.

The important rivers Taw and Teign rise on the north moor, and the north-west corner is the highest part. There are fewer people out walking than on more southerly parts, which are nearer larger population centres. I went in all weathers, particularly loving it when the weather made it feel wilder: on days of wind, snow or sub-zero temperatures.

I often followed the River Taw towards its source, which involved crossing a huge marsh surrounded by higher ground and grazed by livestock and ponies. My favourite walk approached the marsh from above, from where it looked like a poor man's version of an African plain, a huge bowl of grassy land dotted with water and animals, so far below me the sheep, cattle and ponies could be mistaken for something more exotic. A little further into this road-less expanse of moorland is the site of a modest memorial to the poet Ted Hughes, who lived in north Devon and loved the moor. A block of granite, simply inscribed with his name, sits on a low mound. It is notoriously difficult to find, barely visible until you are almost on top of it. I missed it many times before finally nearly stumbling over it. The location is so remote, they had to use a helicopter to get the stone there.

Walking this northern part of the moor also brought me close to the army training areas. These are closed to the public when used for firing at times during the week, but are usually open at weekends. The edges are marked by red-and-white poles. Red flags fly when access is not permitted, but troops also use adjacent areas of the moor for other, less lethal forms of training, and I often saw them. Some walkers resent their presence, but I found them an interesting addition to the landscape, wondering what they were up to and what being out there was like for them. Whenever I met them, they were always polite and mostly friendly. Once, out walking in the mist on the moor with my partner Andrew, we sat in a dip by a wall to get out of the wind and eat our sandwiches. As we stood up we heard voices. We climbed up on to the bank in front of it and walked along. As we turned the corner we saw a group of soldiers, also eating their sandwiches, maybe 50 feet from where we had been sitting. They had placed their guns on the top of the slope, pointing at us, while they lay on the bank just below. We had a quick chat with the officer, then nervously picked our way along the path, stepping carefully around the guns, saying hello to them all as we passed.

One time, having sat for twenty minutes on a hilltop, eating my lunch, I nearly fell off my rocky perch when I suddenly noticed an armed soldier crouched 20 feet away, with a rock behind him, his camouflage so good I only saw him when he shifted position. Looking around with new eyes, I saw three others. They didn't acknowledge me and I didn't acknowledge them. Walking away, I soon met more soldiers coming towards me and saw others fanned out and moving up the hill. One group clearly trying to find the other. Hide-and-seek with weapons.

I walked the slopes of northern Dartmoor in all weathers and mostly on my own. I saw it in the silent, freezing cold, when even the streams were frozen over and snow blew in my face, and on days of sudden, violent showers, when I could see the rain or snow coming towards me from miles away – dark curtains rippling wildly in the wind, as I looked around for somewhere to shelter.

Until we moved to live on the southern edge of Dartmoor, trespassing was not something I had done very often. Occasionally, I might have taken a shortcut across a patch of ground I knew I had no right to be on, or lost my way and found it preferable to climb over a gate into a field, rather than retrace my steps; but setting out with the intention of trespassing was new to me. Given the force of the rain that day, I thought it was unlikely anyone would be out, so I set off in reasonable hope of avoiding encounters with potentially unfriendly landowners. I have a low embarrassment threshold and knew I would have no justification for being where I shouldn't; the route I followed was almost certainly once a path to the moor used by local people, but sadly was never made an official footpath.

The rain was so heavy it battered against the hood of my coat and, at times, I was almost up to my ankles in water as I paddled along the road. I stopped to clear the layer of leaves from the roadside drain openings with my foot, risking wet socks to ease the flow down the road a little.

High above the valley, the edge of the moor was softened by low cloud, the pines at the top coming in and out of view. There was no one around. There would have been silence, had it not been for the roar of the river below, the pounding of the rain and the drip and gurgle of water. Everywhere I looked there was movement: gravity on liquid, irresistibly seeking the lowest point.

I walked up the lane and branched off to a footpath, which took me back to the river further up the valley. Here it was steeper and the water was louder and fiercer as it crashed downhill, carrying whatever debris it had encountered on the way. It would hold most of it until it reached the valley floor, the water slowing enough to release its trophies, raising the river bed, sometimes enough to push the water off across our neighbour's fields.

I hopped a fence and squelched upwards into the mist. Suddenly, I was in a beech wood so entrancing I just stopped and stood, absorbing the atmosphere. The trees were old and large. The nearest were a charcoal colour, their trunks wet and dark. Further away, they were lighter by increments, as distance and mist bleached them grey, then silver, then just a ghostly hint of form which could have been imagined. The ground was russet with their leaves, like a flash of colour in a black-and-white film.

I heard a vehicle somewhere. Fearing it might be a landowner approaching on a quad bike, I ducked behind a tree. The sound faded. I stepped out again, walking on saturated grass as I ascended this little upland valley, until I sensed I must be close to a house I had glimpsed previously. To avoid it, I climbed a low fence and stepped on to the edge of the moor, where bramble and bracken were so dense I struggled to get through, grazing and scraping my hands a little in the process. Eventually the vegetation thinned and I climbed the slope on to the moor proper, crossed a small road and entered the marsh, where the river is born.

In retrospect it probably wasn't a good idea to attempt to cross a marsh I didn't know in the pouring rain and mist. There was no path, just giant tussocks of grass acting as stepping-stones above the water. I hopped from one to the other, missing my footing a few times and soaking my boots, inside and out, until I reached what seemed to be the middle – and decided that was far enough.

After growing up in the country, I went to Sussex University near Brighton, before moving to London where, following a bad choice of a master's degree, I couldn't get a job. I temped in a credit card company, entering numbers into a computer, which was one of the worst jobs I have ever had. It required such little concentration we were allowed to wear headphones and listen to music. Never again will I underestimate how exhausting it is to spend all day on a physically undemanding, but mind-numbing task. After a few months of that I still couldn't find anything better, so for the sake of my sanity, found employment in a plant nursery called Rassell's, in Kensington. It occupied what originally must have been intended as the communal garden for the surrounding square of beautiful, white-painted, multi-million-pound houses. A lovely spot, but brutally hard work. The nursery didn't grow much on site, so almost everything had to be brought in and unloaded by hand: plants, compost and pots. I remember no trolleys or other aids, just endlessly carrying stuff. Perhaps trolleys were deemed to be unsuitable, as the paths were cobbled.

When I first experienced the arrival of the lorry loaded with bags of potting compost, I was surprised to see almost everyone else had disappeared. Most of the staff seemed to have suddenly found something essential to do elsewhere, leaving just two of us to unload. At the end of the day I also realised why they'd laughed when I'd asked about the nearest public swimming pool. I had no energy to eat a meal or speak to anyone, let alone go swimming. I got the Tube home and went straight to bed. It got easier as I became fitter, but I rarely had enough energy or time left to take advantage of the lucrative sideline of gardening for the wealthy local residents, who were happy to pay top hourly rates for people who were traceable back to the nursery.

I became obsessed with plants. I was already a frustrated gardener. When I was supposed to be writing essays and revising for my finals at university, I had been struck by an overwhelming compulsion to grow things. I bought seeds, trays and compost and set them up all over the house I shared with two very tolerant housemates. I filled the garden and numerous pots with flowers and it all looked amazing. It was an odd hobby for a twenty-one-year-old, but I was hooked.

When it was quiet at the nursery, I would read the plant books in the little hut that served as shelter and pay point. I didn't have a garden, but desperately wanted one, so bought big pots and plants using my staff discount and somehow carried them home on the Tube from High Street Kensington to Willesden Green, to grow on a little rooftop in the maisonette I shared with my friend Trish and two others. Living below us was the writer Penelope

Mortimer, who had the most beautiful garden, which we overlooked. She had previously had a large garden in the country and this one looked like a miniature version: a central statue flanked by symmetrical flower beds in the form of a half-circle. To one side was a spectacular poplar tree. I thought it was the most stunning tree I had ever seen. The leaves danced with a silver shimmer in the slightest breeze.

Once, she wanted some company on a trip to a garden somewhere off the North Circular Road. She had seen my roof garden, which had escalated from herbs in pots to small trees in large plastic bins, and kindly invited me to come along. I have never been so scared in a car. Everywhere she drove, horns blared at us and I repeatedly thought we were about to crash. On getting out of the car on our arrival back home, I learned the true meaning of the phrase 'legs like jelly'.

Six months of lifting and carrying left me fitter and slimmer, but still broke. I loved working mostly outdoors, surrounded by trees and plants and some interesting people, but I didn't want to be there forever.

Luckily, I found a slightly better paid job in the 'editorial' department of the free ads paper Loot. Not editorial in the usual sense, as the paper contained only adverts, but a team which vetted those ads to prevent anything which contravened the company's policies, or was illegal, from being sold. The main job, however, was answering calls from the public, usually about something which had gone wrong with their advert. Despite not having to pay for this service, many callers were angry when it disappointed. Some were abusive and occasionally there were threats. We also had to deal with those who turned up in person. I once had a man try to climb over the front desk to attack me. I had a caller threaten to kill me more than once. This was obviously alarming, but the rudeness, milder aggression and verbal abuse over the phone was worse because it happened most days. It felt more like a kind of warped therapy line, a telephone punchbag, where people could take out their anger and life frustrations on me and my colleagues.

I felt increasingly anxious as I walked to work along the polluted length of Kilburn High Road, dodging dead pigeons and people gawping at the scene of regular accidents, as well as trying to avoid the mentally-ill black woman who was, I think, Mad Mary, who later featured in Zadie Smith's novel White Teeth. She seemed to hate cyclists: shouting, screaming and spitting at them. I was on foot, so thankfully safe from that. I hated car drivers, whose vehicles pumped out fumes as they inched forward at a slower pace than mine, on foot. Sometimes they shouted at me for daring to cross a side road in front of them, an action which delayed them by seconds from joining the almost stationary queue on the main road. The best thing about Kilburn High Road was a shop I loved to lose myself in on the way home: One World Supermarket. This emporium, run by an Indian couple, was just what it said: food from around the world, from freeze-dried jellyfish to every pulse and spice you could imagine, as well as massive bunches of fresh herbs, three for £1.

Over time, the job caused my stress levels to rise and remain high. I felt as if I was becoming a different person, someone who was constantly on guard and quick to see the worst in anyone and everything. I became cynical, embittered and sad. The benefits offered by the company – primarily free fruit and a daily fifteen-minute massage – were nice, especially the amazing head, hand and shoulder massage, but not enough to overcome my stress for more than a few hours. I desperately needed to get out.

I was still applying for better jobs and was delighted to get an interview at the children's book publisher Usborne. It paid peanuts, but sounded like heaven. The successful applicant would be assigned projects, such as a book about cooking, or growing plants for younger children. They would see it through from actually doing the cooking or growing the plants, to working with experts, to writing the book and getting their name on the cover. I wanted this more than anything in my life. The first step was to complete a task. I think it was three pages of a book on GCSE chemistry. I took two days off work and spent them, and the weekend, writing the text and drawing the illustrations. Then there was an interview, which went well, I thought, but I didn't get the job. A week later, they were back in touch. Another job had come up and they wished to choose between the top two rejected applicants. We had to complete another project. I took another two days off work and put my heart into it. A week later I got the bad news that the other person had got the job. I was devastated. I had a soul-destroying job that barely paid me enough to live in a shared house, and no prospects. I felt constantly anxious and was becoming depressed. I was losing friends because I was hard to be around. I found it tough being around myself, so no wonder others struggled. I was starting to hate London and I felt crushed by failure. The future looked hopeless.

What kept me going through these hard times was planning walking trips away from the city, swimming and political activism. Soon after arriving in London I visited the London Lesbian and Gay Centre in Farringdon, where I saw a notice about a new direct-action group. I attended one of the first meetings of Outrage!, which was set up in response to violence against gay men and lesbians, and the entrapment and arrest of gay men by the Metropolitan Police. I took part in a few of the joyous, theatrical actions organised by the group, including a kiss-in at Piccadilly Circus, held in protest against the arrests of gay men for kissing in public. It seems hard to believe now – when Pride marches regularly feature a police contingent – but in the early 1990s police officers in London were actually arresting men for kissing each other.

I loved being involved in Outrage!, although the meetings were often long and a little dull. I also made a few friends there. It was the rest of gay life in London which was the problem for me. It was quite alienating. I lacked self-confidence and felt awkward in clubs and pubs. I didn't feel I was attractive enough or fitted in. Although I could wear the costume and act the part for a while, it didn't sit comfortably. I wasn't cut out to be an urban gay man – but what other kind of gay man was there? I didn't know, because in my mostly rural childhood in West Wales, there had been no role models at all – and I had never knowingly met anyone gay until I started university. On top of that, the only gay men in view were television personalities and actors like Larry Grayson and John Inman. I couldn't connect with them and certainly didn't want to be them: they were figures of fun. Then, as a young adult living in Brighton and London, gay men were city types. Most of the ones I met didn't seem to like the things I liked. Being gay and living in the country didn't seem to be an option either. I remember pondering with my best friend and housemate Trish where we might be able to live other than London or Brighton. We thought possibly Bristol, maybe Edinburgh, then ran out of ideas. Most of Britain looked closed to us. Our identities had geographical limits.

What made me happy was escaping London and walking in landscapes free of people and pressure. I sought out places where I felt nature was more in charge than man. The things I noticed in the city were those scrubby plots of unused land in the process of being colonised by wild plants, or weeds as some would have it. A patch of weedy flowers on a building site felt like a small triumph against the relentless traffic, car fumes and stony-faced people: nature holding up a sign to say, 'You can't beat me'. I looked for free-willed wildness at the sides of railway lines, in the larger 'parks' like Hampstead Heath, Wanstead Flats and Richmond, and anywhere neglected. Most gay men would probably have been interested in the rampant action in the undergrowth in places like that. I wasn't brave enough, so was more likely to be looking at the trees. Although later in my life (in Cornwall of all places) I did pluck up the courage to sample that kind of gay life.

On trips out of London, I became obsessed with a search for places which felt wild, those bits of un-farmed land: the heaths, flower meadows, verges and woodlands which had escaped the plough and the improver. I sought them out and spent time in them. I dreamed of leaving the city permanently, but didn't know how.

Sitting on the train, watching the view, my eyes swept past the farmed fields to the woods and heaths. Travelling south or south-west my heart lifted when the houses and roads of London became more scattered, then stopped. I'd look for the track-side remnants of sandy heathland in Surrey and Hampshire, colonised by birch trees, shining with gorse flowers. I had read Thomas Hardy and I imagined those heaths stretching from horizon to horizon, a blend of wild and grazed, a place where humans were secondary to nature, a place of sanctuary for those who understood and wanted that.

I remembered the excitement of finding orchids on the edge of the lawn at my childhood home, and how gutted I felt when my father pushed the mower over them. I was once a little boy who loved flowers, birds and animals. I used to pick wild flowers in the woods to give to people, until I learned that walking around with a bunch of primroses was a red flag to a bully.

I started reading books about the countryside. I bought The History of The Countryside and Trees and Woodland in the British Landscape by Oliver Rackham. I read how much we had lost, how little ancient woodland was left, how the vast majority of heathland in Britain had disappeared. I heard about the inspiring campaigns against the building of the M11 link road in East London and the M3 extension at Twyford Down. This seemed the same battle to me, a young man turning asthmatic from breathing car fumes and grieving the destruction of the countryside. I briefly became a volunteer in the offices of an organisation supporting these campaigns.

I took day trips to the edges of London, to see the ancient trees of Epping Forest, the stately beech woods of the Chilterns, the Essex coast, where salt marsh blurred the line between land and sea, and the Surrey hills and North Downs, with views across the Weald so stunning it looked like one vast forest, as once it was. I also discovered how far I could get from London on a day trip. There was a fast train which stopped at the village of Brockenhurst in the New Forest. In a little over one-and-a-half hours I could be in the middle of one of the richest woodland landscapes in Europe. If I got up early enough, I could have a full day in its mix of dense woods, areas of pasture studded with magnificent old oaks and open heathland. Just five minutes from the busy car park on the edge of this village, it was possible to be the only person on a path, to see a deer and fawn, or disturb a herd, then watch it flow over a fence, like water over a rock in a stream.

I had always loved trees. It would surely be a strange person who doesn't. But, where I grew up in west Wales, tree cover was much lower than in many parts of Britain, and woods were mostly small and scrubby. I don't remember seeing many older trees, apart from some magnificent churchyard yews. A big and ancient tree was, therefore, an exotic and entrancing sight for me. It was a thrill to know the tree before me had seen the Victorian era, or the oak whose rough and fissured trunk I was touching might have been a sapling at the time of the English Civil War.

The New Forest really opened my eyes to the beauty of trees, perhaps because I had never seen so many in one place. This wasn't like the wet Welsh woods I played in as a child, where it was hard to distinguish one tree from another in the tangle of saplings and scrub. Here were giant oaks in woodland pastures, stretching broader than they were tall into the graceful shapes they become when given room.

I became adept at organising my twenty or so days of holiday around the concept of the short break, so I could escape as often as possible. Taking Fridays and/or Mondays off was the most time-efficient way to do this. My life revolved around these trips. I went walking on the moors of the Derbyshire Peak District, the heathland and coast of Dorset, the woods of the New Forest and the mountains of Wales. Sometimes I went with a friend, but often I went alone.

In Dorset I travelled by train and bus to stay in cheap B&Bs in Wareham or on the Isle of Purbeck, completing all-day, circular walks on the heathlands around Poole Harbour and the remnants of the heaths to the north-west.

Climbing above the trees to the top of Woolsbarrow Fort, in what is now marked on maps as Wareham Forest (a vast area of mostly depressing conifer plantations), I got a sense of what Hardy must have seen: mile upon mile of semi-wild heathland stretching all the way to the sea, so impressive it deserved to be a character in its own right. Now, most of it felt dead, suffocated by these light-excluding, alien conifers, planted because heathland had no value to people who only saw the countryside as an income generator. Much of it would once have been common land, used by local people to graze animals and collect fodder and firewood. Those rights mostly disappeared long ago and planting conifers, or ploughing it up, gave a point to something otherwise pointless in a world of pound signs. This isn't just a modern attitude. Old maps often name scrub and heathland, land of little commercial value, as 'waste'.

Considering Dorset has lost more of its heathland than it has left, it's surprising that south of Wareham there were still larger, more intact areas of heath, including Arne, owned by the RSPB, and big stretches around Studland. Walking on these remnant heaths on the edges of Poole Harbour in the early 1990s, I was heartened to see attempts were being made to restore small sections on the edges, to reclaim them from 'progress' and make them 'waste' again. A sign announcing 'heathland restoration' on a scrubby patch of land was one of the first times I had seen the situation moving in the opposite direction, away from destruction and loss. I took a photo of the sign and put it in an album I made of my trips.

Early one March morning I caught a train from London Euston for my first solitary walking trip. Still half-asleep, I dozed a little, then changed on to increasingly smaller, emptier trains, before eventually arriving at my destination on the south side of the estuary of the River Mawddach in north Wales. The landscape had become wilder and more mountainous as the train approached the borders of Snowdonia (now known as Eryri National Park). Great granitic outcrops of rock dominated the view, bigger and harder than any farmer could destroy.

Expecting a station, I stepped down on to what was little more than a concrete slab surrounded by fields. I was greeted by lambs, attracted perhaps by the warmth of the concrete in the sun. There were no buildings and there was no one else there. As the train headed off towards the bridge across the river to Barmouth, the only sound I heard was bleating. I looked around. West was the sea, north was the wide river mouth and beyond that a range of mountains. East and south were more mountains – the stunning range that includes Cadair Idris, just under 3,000 feet, which I planned to cross the following day.

I walked up into the foothills until I reached two beautiful lakes, Llynnau Cregennen, from where I followed a path in parallel with the vast Mawddach estuary far below, to the youth hostel where I was to stay. That evening, not much wanting company, I walked into a wood of twisted oaks high above the river and watched the sun fall slowly into the Irish Sea through the silhouetted branches. The day before I had been in London, mentally exhausted after a hard week at an office on the Kilburn High Road, where traffic fumes were sometimes thick enough to be visible, a bluish and toxic haze. Now, I was gazing through clean air at a landscape more beautiful than any I had ever seen.

When I woke the following day, it was raining; not a drizzle but a downpour. I had no choice but to set off. I'd booked another youth hostel for that night at a place called Corris, the other side of Cadair Idris. I looked up at the mountain. There was nothing to be seen: the cloud had dropped almost as low as the hostel. I was not a confident enough map reader to attempt walking an unfamiliar mountain in those conditions. I would have to go round.

Before I left, I had roughly worked out how far I could happily walk in a day and booked places to stay accordingly. I hadn't thought of having to change my route. Walking round the mountain would at least double the distance, as I wanted to walk as little as possible on busy roads, and the footpath alternatives took less direct routes.

Despite being clad head to foot in waterproofs, with drybags protecting my clothes inside my rucksack, I grew steadily wetter. In some respects it was a miserable walk, or it could have been, had I decided to see it like that. From my perspective, however, it was an adventure, and I was happier out on the Welsh hills in torrential rain, with a 20-mile or more walk ahead of me, than in a soul-shrivelling office in London. I wasn't just putting up with it, I was enjoying it. I felt free. I had no choice but to take each moment as it came, with a vague plan to get from A to B. Of course, a route combining footpaths, minor roads and faint tracks on a map was not reliable on a day when gentle streams had turned into monstrous torrents. I had to revise the route several times to avoid streams I could not cross, sometimes having to walk a long way uphill to find a place I could jump over, or safely wade through. I lost my way; a lot.

It was slightly frightening, very exciting and absolutely exhausting. The landscape was alive with water, pouring from the sky, down the hills and cascading from the mountains. I didn't meet anyone. Eventually I made it to the main road and walked on the verge as best I could. Finally, I escaped the cars and stepped on to the first of several more footpaths, followed by a few more climbs and right-of-way puzzles and an eternity of sodden trudging. When I finally stumbled into Corris, it was almost dark and I was beyond tired.

I was met by the woman who looked after the hostel. Not only did I have it to myself, but this amazing place had a drying room equipped with a dehumidifier, where all my clothes, my boots and most of the contents of my rucksack could be spread out and were dry by morning. It also had a living area with a log fire, which she lit for me. I was high on endorphins and a massive sense of achievement. I slept well.

The next day I ached all over and had to move carefully to start, so took things slowly, gently walking the last stretch of my trip on minor roads and footpaths, between mountains and through woods, to Machynlleth, where I had time to look around before catching my train home.

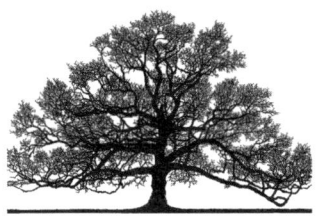

Walking

I didn't find 'real' walking until I was well into my twenties, not long before I moved to London. Obviously, I'd been for walks, but not long ones, unless there was a destination I could only get to on foot.

These days, if I don't know what to do with myself, one of the best things I can do is walk. If I feel stuck, walking often helps. If I need to think about something, walking can focus my mind. As sleep and dreams are a way for the brain to process life, so walking enables me to have silent conversations with myself and process my thoughts. I try to find time to walk every morning before I start my day. Occupying part of my mind with the mechanics of movement, and the attention necessary to prevent myself from tripping up, frees the rest to solve a problem, or just mentally wander. Sometimes, by just letting my thoughts drift softly over something while I move, something positive happens.

Movement is also a release for frustrations, both large and

small. Exercise can change my mood, but there's also something about the simple act of moving forward which is positive, no matter what else in life is not. Sometimes I meet someone I know, or see something remarkable. Occasionally I meet someone new and have an interesting chat. I always feel like I have achieved something. I don't think I have ever regretted going for a walk, long or short.

Before I moved to London and personal difficulties forced me to find new ways of coping (mainly spending time walking in nature) I had no idea that something as simple as going for a walk, or a swim, or – for those who like that sort of thing, playing some kind of sport – when done repeatedly, could change mood, outlook and life.

As an adolescent, I put walking in the same basket as sport, which I hated with a passion. At school I endured cross-country runs (though they were far better than the alternative, which was usually rugby). Our PE teacher used to make us jump up and down before starting the run, so that any boxes of matches would rattle and be discovered, but, of course, we simply hid a few matches and the cigarettes down our legs, inside our socks .

I didn't just hate sport because I was useless at it, but because it came with a load of macho baggage against which I instinctively recoiled. Hearing my father's hate-filled shouting at a rugby match on the television, or enduring the changing rooms at school, was enough to put anyone off.

I had zero motivation in team sports. I couldn't have cared less whether my team won or not. The 'team' in this case would have been put together just five minutes earlier, so it always puzzled me how the others could develop a loyalty to it so quickly. All I cared about was not getting hurt and it being over with as quickly as possible. In primary school, my friend Robert and I got into trouble for making up our own rules for playing football when we were forced to. Rule number one was you had to be as far away as possible from the ball at all times.

The point of rugby at my state grammar school was for the school team for each year group to get practice. A 'seconds' team therefore needed to be cobbled together to play against them: sacrificial victims picked from the leftovers. I spent my time trying, and failing, to look like I cared about the game, while hoping the ball wouldn't come anywhere near me. Why would I want it, when I knew the result would be half a ton of teenage boys hurling themselves in my direction? Each term I carefully dealt out a slim pack of excuses, my 'get-out-of-games-free' cards. They were regularly shuffled and not repeated too frequently: I felt unwell, so had to go to the sick room, I had forgotten my kit or I was ill at home so couldn't go to school at all that day. Astonishingly, this whole enforced sports thing went on into the final two years. I escaped it by taking extra lessons for an O-Level in German, which mercifully took place in the games slot. The year before that I had somehow dredged up enough courage to tell the PE teacher, a large and intimidating man, that I wasn't able to play rugby any more. I have no idea what reason I gave, but I remember he just looked at me and said, 'Alright'. If only I'd had the courage to do that earlier.

If walking in walking boots was a thing back in the 1970s, I didn't know about it. As a child in Milford Haven, an oil port just outside the Pembrokeshire Coast National Park, my family, and the people we knew, might go for a stroll on the cliff path, or take the dog for a walk, but walking as a pursuit was something done by others.

I clearly remember them, the figures swathed in waterproofs, bearing rucksacks, trudging through what must have seemed an industrial blot on the otherwise stunning and recently opened

186-mile path along the Pembrokeshire coastline. From where I stood, they looked like aliens, so ridiculously unlike anyone around them that I wanted to laugh. From their side, they must have wished there was a shuttle bus of some kind to whisk them past the oil refineries, tankers and terraced houses. They certainly didn't look like they were enjoying the view, and to be honest, it wasn't that pretty – but I didn't know that at the time.

Milford is magnificent in many ways. It is in the top ten of the world's largest natural harbours, has houses you can buy for astonishingly little compared to most places on the coast of southern Britain, and is a shortish drive from some of the best beaches you've ever seen. When I went to university in Brighton I couldn't believe it that people travelled from London to sit on hard pebbles next to a sea that was more often brown or pewter in colour, rather than blue or green.

When I lived in Milford it was a fiercely working-class place – and I wasn't. For me, it was a town dominated by bullies and men who drank a lot. It had pubs a-plenty, the streets were deserted when Wales played rugby and I was able to walk to school and back alone as a six-year-old.

My parents retired to a bungalow in Hakin, the western half of the town. It faced west and the view from their living room on the inland cliffs was of the sun setting into the water beyond the Heads, the limits of the haven, perhaps four or five miles away, out where the sea was to be feared. After my mother's death, when the house was sold, you could barely have bought a flat in south Devon for the price. Milford has its own beauty, but is a predominantly grey town, with high deprivation and a high street which used to be a thriving, busy place, but now looks very sad.

As a child I lived in a new house on a new road, next to a potato field. I would dash in after the pickers had finished, and get whatever they'd missed. My mother gave me five pence a bucket and we'd eat these delicious things for weeks. Years later I tried being a proper picker with a friend. The pay was good, but it was extremely hard work. Hilariously, we two fifteen-year-olds combined were no match for the one older woman working the next row, even though her row was longer than ours.

Above the field was a large area of scrubland, full of brambles, long grass and ragwort crawling with cinnabar moth caterpillars, striped yellow and black like the uniform tie for the grammar school I would later attend. Through the scrub were paths leading to a nineteenth-century fort, a place of terror and excitement, with huge surrounding walls, an open central area and rooms we thought of as 'dungeons' below ground. The fort overlooked the waterway and led down to a pebbly beach called Gelliswick. These places, and the woods and little beach called Conduit, pronounced Cunjick for some reason, were my playground: making dens, swinging on ropes suspended from trees, running away from bullies, picking blackberries, riding bikes. Cunjick was where I later scattered my father's ashes in sight of the pilot's jetty he once fell from while drunk, and nearly drowned. As I got older, I'd walk into town, a long trek, unless I wanted to take a shortcut across the docks and chance being caught by the dock police. Once, when I was very young, perhaps seven or eight, my friends and I walked all the way from Milford along the coast to the nearest nice beach, called Sandy Haven. I remember it was a slog. Walking for me was about getting somewhere. It wasn't pleasurable.

For most of my childhood my parents were at war. Their relationship was fiery. My father was an alcoholic, who became gradually worse as I grew up. He was away at sea when I was small, working his way up the ranks on ships travelling all over the world, but particularly to ports in the Baltic Sea, the Mediterranean and the Persian Gulf. When his ship docked in Britain, but he was unable to come home, we would sometimes travel to Hull, or Southampton, or London, to visit him. I loved all the attention I got from the crew, who perhaps enjoyed seeing me because they were missing their own families. I remember them building me a pyramid of beer cans so I could shoot at them with my suction cup dart gun. It now seems ironic that I so enjoyed the by-products of what was probably the start of his drinking problem. I imagine they all drank a lot. I was recently given a letter my father wrote to his brother when he was eighteen. Most of it was about getting drunk. He proudly boasted about passing out with a glass in his hand, falling on it and badly cutting his hand.

By the time I was eight or nine my father was what might be called a functioning alcoholic. He would be sober, I hope, when working as a pilot guiding ships as big as 250,000 tons into the haven, but disappeared to the pub for much of the rest of the time. His job gave him plenty of time to indulge his drinking; he was on call for piloting for twenty-four hours, then off for forty-eight. By the time we moved to an isolated house in the country, things were really bad. I now wonder why my parents made that move. Perhaps my mother thought he'd be further away from pubs? It didn't work, if that was her motivation.

She had yet to start going to Al-Anon meetings, for family members of alcoholics, where she learned how powerless she was to stop his drinking and how she needed to concentrate on looking after herself. Before that, she was a demonstrably and understandably angry person. She threw away drink she found in the house, locked him out if he wasn't back when he said he would be and shouted at him a lot. This tended to escalate the situation.

One night I was woken by the sound of breaking glass. I went towards the front door to find my father trying to smash his way in with an axe. My mother had locked him out. The glass in the door had shattered, he had cut himself quite badly and there was blood everywhere. Another time I intervened, aged perhaps twelve, as he attacked my mother. He turned on me. I ran away into the woods until it started to get dark, when I realised I had no choice but to go back, as there was nowhere else to go. The day before the first of my A-Level exams something snapped in me and I stood up to him, perhaps because I dreamed of leaving and was on the verge of doing so. He slapped me repeatedly around the face and head. I told no one. I wanted to, but didn't know who to talk to. I had a little motorbike at that time and drove it to the house of a woman, a potter, who I thought I might be able to tell. I sat outside for a bit, but couldn't quite make myself go in. Somehow, the next day, I went to school, sat my exams and ended up with three 'A' grades.

My father frequently picked me up from school drunk, the car veering from one side of the lane to the other, me fearing we would crash at any minute. Once, while a friend was visiting, we watched as he drove his car home down the drive and just kept going, crashing into the wall of a flower bed. We laughed, but I wasn't laughing inside.

He nearly died several times. His car, an embarrassing three-wheeled Robin Reliant, went out of control on a hill, crashed into a wall at speed and disintegrated, but he was thrown out. He broke many bones and was almost entirely covered with paint which splattered out of the tins he'd stored in the back of the car for use on his boat. As he proudly pointed out many times ... if he had been wearing a seat belt, he would have died.

He fell into the freezing sea one February after leaving the pilot boat drunk and slipping on the metal jetty, but someone saw him and pulled him out in time. He subsequently lost his job. He was finally banned from driving. He temporarily stopped drinking without medical help and suddenly one day had a violent and terrifying alcohol withdrawal fit in the living room. He had stomach cancer. He had liver failure, jaundice and internal haemorrhaging. I didn't recognise him when I went to see him in hospital and the consultant told me he would die soon, but he didn't. He finally succumbed to cirrhosis of the liver and died at the age of seventy. There were perhaps three or four years in his sixties, after losing his job, in which he didn't drink. He bought an old boat and restored it, and went on holidays with my mother. I was pleased for her, but didn't trust him to stay sober.

The first casualty in an alcoholic household is honesty; the second, reliability. You could never depend on my father to do anything. Outside the house he was a popular man. Everybody seemed to like him. Inside, he was a racist, homophobic drunk, who made promises he rarely kept. I think he drank so he didn't have to face his fears and failures, so he could put a lid on it all and have a good time with his cronies in the pub. But I also think he was genetically predisposed to become an alcoholic, something my brother sadly inherited, dying from a heart attack in his early sixties.

My father's brother kept a newspaper cutting about him, which I'd never seen until it arrived last year in a bundle of photographs from my cousin Nicola, after the death of my Uncle David. It relates a shocking incident which happened one dark December day when my father was living at home with his parents, working as an apprentice pilot in Barry. It seems he had been shadowing an experienced pilot, who had taken a ship from Barry out into the Bristol Channel, two miles from shore. Both of them were then picked up from the ship by a pilot boat. Transferring from one to the other is perhaps the most dangerous moment in that job, as the pilot often has to descend a ladder from the ship and sometimes jump on to the deck of the pilot boat. The ladder descent is often very lengthy, as the outward-travelling ships will mostly have unloaded their cargoes and be sitting higher in the water. My father had jumped on to the pilot boat safely, but the pilot Charles Peterson lost his footing as he tried to do the same, and fell in the sea. My father was commended for managing to throw a lifebuoy 20 yards to land over Mr Peterson's shoulders. Presumably it had a rope attached, as he then pulled the man back to the boat and caught hold of his wrist. Another man sat on my father's ankles as he reached down to try to help the pilot from the water. This proved impossible and the report states the pilot said, 'I am done – I am going', before slipping from my father's grasp. Despite a two-hour lifeboat search he was not found until his body washed up days later. The inquest was told my father did not think the man could swim. The most upset I ever saw my father was when, years after this event (of which I knew nothing), one of his fellow pilots in Milford also died after falling between a ship and the pilot boat while disembarking.

Nobody was allowed to acknowledge my father's alcoholism, or even that he drank too much, or had been drinking on any particular occasion, without him becoming enraged and occasionally violent. It was like living with a dangerous wild animal. If my mother or I even hinted at anything of the sort, he would laugh and, in words so slurred you could barely understand them, deny he had touched a drink that day. If you pushed it any further there would be trouble. I mostly avoided physical violence, but on the night before my first A-Level exam, it was simply stating the obvious fact that he was drunk, and not backing down, which led to him hitting me.

He was ridiculously, sentimentally affectionate to pets when drunk, but never had anything nice to say to me. Maybe the bad memories have pushed anything nice so far to the back of my mind

I can't remember them. I don't remember him saying 'Well done' when I did well at school, or taking any interest in what I was reading or my latest hobby. I hated having to help him fix up his boat, which was more about having to spend time with him than about what we were doing. He thought I hadn't picked up the feel for carpentry he imagined he had inherited from his grandfather, who was a joiner. The only memory I have of him seeming pleased or proud was when I started tuition at school to take the Oxbridge entrance exam. I soon decided Oxford and Cambridge were the last universities I would choose, as their courses seemed old-fashioned compared to Sussex, but that might also have been to spite him.

My mother had a difficult life with him. She sometimes had bruises ... and when I was about nine, they announced they would divorce. It probably would have been better if they had. Of course, I was also a casualty of the situation, although I didn't know it at the time. It was hard for my mother and I supported her as much as I could, but she wasn't an easy person either, quick to lose her temper and often so consumed by her difficult marriage and poor health, she had no space to hear or see my problems. My childhood was tricky in those respects, but it was also privileged, as they had enough money most of the time – and I lived in a beautiful place.

I knew about landscapes and the power of nature. I knew places on the coast which were so breathtakingly beautiful they made me feel small. Places worth the walk. I loved standing on top of the Preseli Hills in North Pembrokeshire on a clear day, with a view all the way to north Wales, and west across the sea to what must have been the Wicklow Mountains in Ireland. When the wind was up I loved to be on the Preselis. I also loved a storm on the coast, watching gigantic waves crash on the rocks, or standing with my arms out, leaning forward, held upright by the force of the wind.

My job in the evening was to watch the weather forecast for my father, while he helped get dinner ready, if he was sober enough to do so. I became familiar with wind speeds and their direction. The gales could be so fierce they once made the windows in our house visibly flex, and my father warned me to keep away from them for fear they would blow in. Another time I had to help a friend push her bike up the hill from our house. It was so windy, she couldn't do it on her own. As we struggled past one of the nearby building plots, a workman's hut blew apart like an explosion and its contents took flight, luckily not in our direction.

After my father died, I felt nothing – not even the anticipated regret at losing any chance of reconciling with him. I listened as my grieving mother tried to resurrect him as a decent man with an illness we should forgive. I tried to find some positive memories. I remembered him not slowing down when driving over humpbacked bridges because I loved it when the bump lifted me off my seat in the back. I liked going to the beach with him in the lifeboat he converted to have beds and a galley, with a wooden frame over the engine making a table from which to eat my mother's spaghetti bolognese; me and my friends, sandy, sunburned and happy after a day on the beach at Watwick, where I later scattered her ashes on the path down, as she had requested. I most liked it when the sea was rough and the boat climbed up and fell down the swells, like going over a hundred humpbacked bridges.

I noticed the seals, the little fish that nibbled your legs, the blue-black sheen of mussels, the transparent jellyfish with streaks of brilliant colour, the dolphin which once spent a summer off the beach, and the immense tankers, perhaps guided by my father, as they passed on their way to or from the jetties for the oil refineries visible to the east. Years later I returned one Christmas to stay on St Ann's Head above Watwick in a house whose front windows faced the industrial sprawl of Milford Haven, while the rear ones looked towards the bird reserve islands of Skokholm and Skomer, names betraying the part played by Vikings in the history of Pembrokeshire more than a thousand years ago. At night the whole haven to the east was lit up with the jetty and refinery lights, while the west was dark and silent.

The gannets came from another Pembrokeshire island with a Viking name, Grassholm, the furthest offshore. You could see it from the coast path sometimes, 10 miles away, shining like a beacon with the white bodies of tens of thousands of these huge, sleek and graceful birds. We would walk to St Ann's Head and look to see if the distant island of Lundy was visible, far to the south, almost as far as Cornwall.

I drew islands and added mountains and forests, towns and villages. I made up names for them and imagined the people who lived there. I dreamed about them. On the beach I would choose a rock and turn it into my own island, building little sand and shell houses, walls of stone and woods of seaweed. I would watch with a mixture of fear and fascination as the tide crept up the sides. How easily what we value can be destroyed. How vulnerable we all are in the end.

We went mushroom picking on an abandoned airfield above West Dale beach, walking the coast path to get to it, looking forward to the mushroom soup my mother would make. We gathered cockles from a sandy estuary and buckets of blackberries from hedgerows. My mother was unusual for the far west of Wales in the 1970s, reading Schumacher's Small is Beautiful, treating herself with herbal medicines, nettles and dandelion leaves, making paella in a huge pan with the cockles and mussels we'd collected, and growing vegetables, some of which were so exotic at that time, you couldn't even buy them locally: aubergines, courgettes, peppers and tomatoes that she turned into ratatouille and her own bottled tomato sauce.

Walking

When I became a boy who lost himself in books, my mother, daughter of a bricklayer, who grew up on a council estate in Barry and left school at fifteen, went to adult education classes to learn about the classics of English literature so she could help me. She played bridge and once played for Wales. She made gardens and grew unusual plants, loved pottery and colour.

She was proudly Welsh, refusing to stand up at the annual prize-giving at the grammar school when 'God Save The Queen' was played first, before the Welsh national anthem. She sometimes voted for Plaid Cymru, the Welsh nationalist party. She could also alter her accent to suit the situation: more Welsh among people with stronger accents, less among those who sounded more English. She had a strong sense of justice and felt people should stand up for each other. She once went to my primary school to protest at a new approach to taking the register in the mornings: one or more children were chosen to stand on their chairs and report on anyone seen talking. My mother asked the headmaster whether the next step would be for the children to be asked to wear black shirts. There was no more standing on chairs and snitching.

On the day of her funeral, not so many years ago, my heart tearing apart, some childhood friends and I went back to another beach, Sandy Haven, where we spent so much time together, where our mothers drank cups of tea from flasks as we went cockling and catching crabs at low tide. Middle-aged, we stood looking at the dark water and the woods as the light fell, and a multitude of crows flew raucously along paths across the sky to their night roost on the opposite bank. Noise ... then silence.

As a young man at university in Brighton I was lost. I'd imagined it would be full of people like me, but really I had no idea who I was, except that I liked reading books, was left wing and had a big secret. I studied English with French. In my first French class I think I was the only one who didn't have either a French parent, a home in France or lived part of the year in a French-speaking country. At school I'd been good at the language, but quickly realised this was a different league. The French I'd been taught at school was mostly grammar. My spoken French was dreadful.

My next-door neighbour in halls introduced herself as Jonquil Farquhar, sounding like a character in a girls' book about boarding schools. I went to an event for new first-year students, found no one to talk to and fled in a panic (which is how I still feel in any situation which could be described as 'networking'). I might have been middle class enough in Milford for the bullies from the council estate to target me – my father had a good job and we lived in a nice house – but at university there were kids whose parents were seriously wealthy. Their private school confidence was enviable, and intimidating.

I met two working-class girls in their final year, Jenny and Clare, who were amazing: funny, left wing and saw the world in a way I could relate to. They made me laugh and helped me cope. I came out to them and a few others. I ended my relationship with Sarah, my girlfriend of several years, who was also my best friend. She was understandably upset to discover why. I couldn't really share with her how awful I felt.

Everything became too much. I couldn't cope in seminars. I was anxious all the time and couldn't think straight. I had no self-confidence and felt painfully self-conscious. I had no idea how to write an essay. I could barely speak in seminars, I just clammed up and my head filled with blankness. My tutor allowed me to opt out of classes and spend a term reading books about being gay, which was kind of him, but it might have been better to have helped me learn how to plan a presentation and deliver it.

Struggling to cope with university, being lonely and having just come out were all made worse, I think, by the after-effects of years of living in an alcoholic household. At home I had found ways to cope with it, up to a point, but, ironically, having escaped from home, it seemed to affect me more. I also couldn't sleep because the halls were just a twenty-four-hour party. The kitchen for the corridor was below those on the upper floors and, after a few weeks, you couldn't see out of the window as it was plastered with cooking waste casually emptied from the kitchens above. I slept with a fellow first-year student, who told me the man he was seeing had told him he ought to sleep with other men to get some experience. I needed friendship and affection, but didn't find much of it. I had what some people might call a breakdown. I became mentally allergic to the campus. Off it, I didn't feel too bad, but as soon as I walked from the station towards it, my head filled with white noise and fear.

I started seeing a counsellor, who managed to get me moved to the post-graduate flats, where life was more civilised and quieter, and there was somewhere to sit and eat other than your bed. When I moved in, a friendly American woman called Lori explained that everyone put a few pounds a week into a kitty, which paid for bread, milk, butter, eggs and other basics, and sometimes they ate together. I nearly burst into tears. We became friends and travelled around Ireland together that summer.

I went to the Duke of York's cinema in Brighton to see the ground-breaking film My Beautiful Laundrette at least three times. It felt like the first time I'd ever seen anything about being gay that I could really relate to on screen. My schoolfriend Neil came with me one time, supportive and kind to his newly gay pal. I went on marches to support the miners' strike, against the Thatcher government's Section 28 culture war on gay men and lesbians, against apartheid in South Africa and against cuts to student grants. Walking with others with a purpose.

My first Gay Pride march in London ended up being led by miners and their families, many of whom were Welsh, who had arrived on coaches in their hundreds to thank the gay community, especially the Lesbian and Gay Support the Miners groups, for their support during the recent strike. It was an extraordinary and deeply moving sight, one captured at the end of the 2014 film Pride. They were the last people I would have expected to support gay rights. It showed me what solidarity can achieve.

It wasn't until several years later that I discovered walking for the pleasure of exercise and being outside in nature. My friend Trish and I went to spend Christmas in a rented cottage with two other friends, near a village called Cynghordy, between the Brecon Beacons and what are sometimes called the Cambrian Mountains, or the Green Desert: an area of higher ground running up the middle of Wales. There are photos of me in my Brighton clothes, looking as out of place there, in my suede jacket, as those walkers in Milford did to me when I was a child. I didn't even have walking boots. I'd never owned any. I must have taken ordinary shoes and slipped my way around the countryside. I loved everything about it: the winter landscape, the colours, the space and the clean air. Nights were cold and frosty and there was an open fire to sit beside.

I soon bought some walking boots and, eventually, when we started earning and had both moved to London, Trish and I started going away for weekends, and for a week at Christmas, to beautiful places: to Gillingham in Dorset, where we visited her old school as it was being turned into flats, walking in the sunshine through the bluebells; to North Norfolk in the winter, where the beaches were full of birds and even half a mile inland was riven by channels which filled with seawater at high tide – an unsettling landscape I could relate to, being neither one thing nor another. We went to stay near Beddgelert in Snowdonia, exploring the mountains and the mossy, old Welsh woods. Trish had to go back to London before the end of the week, so I had a few days on my own there. This was when I first realised the power of solitary walking. I got up very early and walked all day, climbing mountains, passing farmers working in the fields, Welsh-speaking men and women whose English had a hesitancy, making me think speaking it was something they didn't do that often. I walked and walked, wearing myself out for the joy of being somewhere stunning. I felt drunk on beauty and exercise. I took a photo of myself in my walking gear in front of the upland cottage we'd rented. When I had the film developed, I realised how fit I had become.

In America I walked with my friend Emily, who had shared the maisonette with me and Trish in London for almost a year. We drove to the Sierra Nevada from her parents' home near San Francisco. It was November, when the days were warm and the nights frosty in the mountains. It was the first time I had travelled outside Europe and I'd never been anywhere with 'wilderness'. The names were so enticing and exotic: Granite Chiefs Wilderness, Desolation Wilderness, Volcanoville, Truckee, Dogtown. We climbed Mount Rose in Nevada, a 10,000-foot snow-covered peak. We got to the snowline too late in the day. As we took photos at the top, the sun was setting. It was beautiful, but we had to get down before dark. Walk turned to run, as we were forced to jog across scree slopes. It was nothing for Emily, who was an athlete and super-fit, but back at her parents' house I felt ill and could do nothing for hours.

Sarah and I became friends again and I went with her on

weekends away in the Brecon Beacons, in the New Forest in the cold and frost and on the Purbeck heaths in Dorset, laughing and walking. I went to Derbyshire for a long weekend, arriving before the friend who was joining me from Manchester. I walked from Edale up into the hills on a sunny evening. I sat by a stream and had a rush of joy so intense it could have been mistaken for a religious experience. Like an epiphany, it made me realise I couldn't go on living in a city. I would still be suffocated by it, even if I had a job I enjoyed.

I went back to Pembrokeshire for a four-day walk one autumn with my friend Chris, who also shared our house in London, a man with a beautiful singing voice. Two gay men in the countryside, we walked from Fishguard along the north coast, staying in B&Bs and sleeping soundly after exercise and a pint or two of beer. I didn't know about singing to seals, but he did. The weather was gorgeous, the path was easy and, all around St David's Head, the seals were close inshore, some seemingly just exploring, others on isolated and inaccessible beaches tending their pups. One day as we descended into a little cove, where the path ran just above the water, Chris spotted a seal's head pop up. He started singing. As he continued, more heads appeared, until he had an audience of ten or more, pushing themselves up out of the water to get a better view, their dog-like faces whiskered and curious.

Gradually, I learned walking was both a stress reducer, a mind calmer and something I could always do if frustrated: until one day, years later, when – suddenly – I couldn't walk any more.

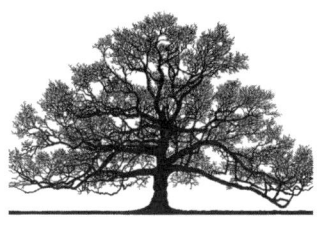

Cornwall

When I lived in London working at jobs which gave me little fulfilment, or money, I knew I needed to do something creative, but I didn't know what, or how. I looked for evening classes in some practical kind of art or craft and settled on pottery. After paying for a term, I went once, found it difficult, didn't like it and, sadly, never went back. Perhaps it was too hard to sustain an evening class while doing a difficult full-time job. I started painting patterns on glass at home, decorating storage jars and making images on pieces of glass which I edged with lead tape, like little stained-glass windows. Other than that, creativity for me was limited to cooking and gardening in pots on my roof terrace.

When I finally escaped from London and moved to Cornwall, I felt like I had landed in heaven. I lived at first as a lodger in Redruth. I loved the town. It had edges you could see, unlike London, where you can sit on a train for half an hour before the city finally gives way to fields. In Redruth the beautiful moorland hill Carn Brea was visible from almost everywhere, and a three-minute walk from the house took me to a footpath through fields. There were many handsome Victorian buildings, as well as cottages and walls of local granite in all its subtle colours. People were friendly and it had a Cornish sense of priorities. I remember once going to the slightly empty-looking greengrocers a bit after 4 p.m. I looked for courgettes, but couldn't see any. I asked and was told they'd already put them away in the back. Yes, they didn't close till 5 p.m., they acknowledged, but if they waited till then to pack up, they'd never get home.

It was a while before I realised that Redruth sat very low down in the hierarchy of Cornish towns as ranked by people who lived in the county. I remember asking someone if they lived in Redruth. They looked at me as if I'd said something rude, and told me no, they lived in St Agnes, which is a pretty village on the north coast. They might not have liked Redruth, but even compared to some of the most expensive parts of London, it looked good to me.

I had moved to Cornwall to do a postgraduate course in journalism. At that time there were only two places offering the shorter National Council for the Training of Journalists diploma for graduates. One was in Harlow, the other at Cornwall College, Pool, between Redruth and Camborne in west Cornwall. When I went for the interview I stayed in a B&B near the village of Zennor, a few miles west of St Ives. It was quite a distance from Redruth, but looked amazing on the map, with the coast below and moorland above, so I couldn't resist visiting. I managed to fit in a walk on the coast path before the interview, watching the gannets diving for fish. I was smitten before I even got to the college.

I made friends on the course, one of whom was renting a house in St Ives, which was the most beautiful town I'd ever seen. Small, but flanked by two large beaches and complicated enough to get lost in its warren of narrow streets lined with granite houses. The roads had interesting names, such as Wheal Dream and Teetotal Street. It was also full of art galleries, including the magnificent Tate St Ives, which had opened a year or so earlier. Perched above Porthmeor Beach, the architects luckily made sure the view was at least as important a part of the building as the contents. On a visit to that gallery from Devon a few years later, I was privileged to happen on the spectacle of a pod of ten or more bottlenose dolphins chasing a shoal of fish. We had just left the Tate and crossed the road to the beach when we spotted them moving west across the bay, sometimes leaping in the air. We watched for ten minutes as they swam fast, breaking out of the water in graceful arcs, followed by a flock of seabirds. When they reached the far side of the bay, it was clear the fish were cornered. The dolphins began leaping up and diving down in one spot, and the birds also joined in.

Wandering round the many art galleries I started to appreciate abstract art more. Paintings, and mixed media work, evoking the Cornish landscape, the granite and the sea, were everywhere. The colours and textures got into my head and stayed there. I also discovered the sculptor Barbara Hepworth, who lived and worked in St Ives, where her studio and sculpture garden can still be visited. I loved the shapes and textures of her work.

I ended up staying after the course was over. I had written speculatively to weekly papers in places I thought I'd like to live, such as Pembrokeshire, Sussex and Cornwall. Quite a few had jobs and I went to six interviews. I was offered five, probably because I was older, at twenty-nine, than most other applicants, so good value. One of the offers was from The West Briton in Truro. The starting pay was really low, but so was rent in Cornwall at that time. I had been seduced by the cliffs, beaches and seabirds, relaxed attitudes, heaths and moors, and by the fact it felt about as far away from London as could be imagined. It really is a long way in British terms, almost as far as you can go and still be in England. The far west of Cornwall is as far by road from London as is Carlisle. Apart from one trip back in a rented van to retrieve my possessions, I don't think I returned to London for ten years. Just the thought of it made me feel anxious.

Before I arrived in Cornwall to do the journalism course I was fizzing with excitement about living somewhere so beautiful, but also apprehensive about what it would be like to be gay there. Would there be any other gay men or lesbians? I needn't have worried as there were plenty. There was also much more of a community feel than in London. After experiencing the capital's gay club meat market it was refreshing to go to a slightly shabby entertainment centre at a holiday park once a month, I think, for a 'disco', where there were both men and women, and every age from early twenties to at least seventy. It was friendly, unpretentious and fun.

There was even a gay walking group, organised by Martin, whose house in an owl-filled valley near Truro I later shared for a while. When I moved to Falmouth to live as a lodger with a gay couple involved in the Miracle Theatre Company, I became part of a gang of friends. We went to the beach together in the summer, then back to someone's house for food and laughs. They were witty, fun and sometimes outrageous. I had much more of a gay life in Cornwall than London. For perhaps the first time since leaving home, I felt like I fitted in.

I worked at The West Briton for six years. I wondered how I'd get on there being gay. I think I came out to the editor before I took the job, to see how he reacted, but he was fine about it – and so was almost everyone else.

The first few years were wonderful. We had great fun and I loved being a reporter. My work was varied and often interesting. The editor was enthusiastic and encouraging. For one day a week I disappeared off to my patch on the north coast. I was responsible for finding stories in an area stretching from the three-mile-long beach at Perranporth to the little one at Porthtowan and inland towards Truro. In summer I'd put my beach bag in the car, visit people I had got to know, somehow find stories to write, and end the day with a swim in the sea. I also had to endure parish council meetings, which could be extraordinarily dull, though some councils were more friendly and their meetings were almost enjoyable.

Another day I wrote an environment page, which appeared weekly and gave me an excuse to interview experts on sharks and trees, heathland and seabirds. I wrote about farmers whose actions degraded Sites of Special Scientific Interest, plans to establish Marine Protected Areas and a project to set up a lobster hatchery to help repopulate the seas with this valuable shellfish.

I became the main reporter at the magistrates' court, getting to know the lawyers and finding out about forthcoming cases. I enjoyed the challenge of sifting through a stack of council agendas nobody else could face reading, and finding good stories lurking in the driest, most jargon-filled corners.

But, after a few years, it all began to pall. I fell out with the new editor and lost confidence. The pay had barely improved and I was sinking into debt. The shows and events came round and round more quickly, year after year, reminding me I was still there, still badly paid and going nowhere. But, if I wanted to progress up the journalist career ladder, I'd have to leave Cornwall to get a job on a daily paper. I couldn't imagine it.

When I took drugs, albeit mild ones, to get through the boredom of three days at the Royal Cornwall Show, I knew I'd had enough. The first few times I'd enjoyed covering the show: talking to men from the Cornish hinterlands about their caged birds, to little children with giant rabbits and hearing a farmer tell me his cow was a prizewinner because she had 'lovely mammaries'. These novelties soon paled, though, especially since the annual show was very rarely blessed with sun. It usually poured. Animals, tens of thousands of visitors and ankle-deep mud were not a great combination. And, although I grew up in the country, this was not my world.

I hadn't lost my love for the landscape, though. I walked the coast and the Penwith moors. I explored the ancient sites with my wonderful new friend Helen, who was also working at the paper when I first started. We went to the holy wells at Madron, where visitors tie scraps of cloth to the surrounding trees, and the well in a little underground grotto at Sancreed, where the steps down to the water and the rocks around it are rich with a kind of luminous and magical moss, studded with coins and keepsakes placed by believers – in what exactly, I did not know. I loved the Mên-an-Tol, an ancient holed stone on the moor, large enough to crawl through, thought in older times to cure all manner of physical problems. Helen showed me the mysterious two-to-three-thousand-year-old fogous, underground passages with a purpose lost in time. They must have taken a lot of work to excavate and line with stone, and there are several surviving examples in the far west of Cornwall. Were they religious, somewhere to hide or just used to store things? Nobody seemed to have a definitive answer.

I learned about the concept of sacred landscapes. I interviewed a county council archaeologist, who introduced me to the idea that Neolithic people built monuments in geographical relation to a rocky hill, or other landscape feature, that they revered, and sometimes even in ways which echoed its shape. The landscape around a particular hill or rocky tor became a sacred space, rich with burial sites, standing stones, rows and circles which all related back to it. Perhaps, as Philip Marsden pondered in his wonderful book about Cornwall, Rising Ground, these ancestor-conscious people thought their mythologised forebears had actually created these rocky hills or tors, just as they themselves were creating the monuments in homage to them.

I walked the whole coast, in no particular order, and absorbed the beauty and the wildlife. I saw bottlenose dolphins surfing in the waves, riding in on one then flipping back to catch the next. I saw gannets flying low then rising and, wings tucked, hitting the water with speed. I knew they came from Grassholm off Pembrokeshire, travelling miles down the Celtic coast to fish and to remind me where I came from. I watched colonies of kittiwakes and razorbills breeding on the cliffs, flying off and returning with beaks full of fish. One day, while walking on the heathy cliffs near Porthgwarra in the far west, I thought I saw an orca pod, a second's flash of black and white.

One year in the 1990s the crews of fishing boats returning to Falmouth reported being surrounded by an amazing sight a few miles offshore: hundreds of basking sharks. These sharks are not an unusual sight in Cornwall in the spring and summer, but are mostly seen singly, some more than 30 feet long, giant mouths open, hoovering up microscopic marine organisms, though I'd only ever seen them from the beach, huge fins sticking out of the water. This time a combination of temperature and sea conditions were thought to have caused a plankton bloom, attracting large numbers of this shark, the second-largest fish in the world. Soon these gentle creatures began arriving all along the south Cornish coast. Photographers sent extraordinary images to the paper:

sharks swimming over white sands in turquoise waters, as big as the yachts above them.

I wrote about the delicate eelgrass beds in the estuaries of rivers such as the Helford, used by many sea creatures as nurseries, and home to seahorses. I found a marine photographer with some stunning photos of these small and exotic-looking fish. I was not alone in being ignorant of the fact that seahorses were even found in the UK.

I followed efforts to save Cornish heathland, which, like elsewhere, was once a habitat that stretched for miles. There used to be a vast heath that covered much of the middle of the county, a common land whose resources were used by the poor. Now it was reduced to fragments and even those were still seen by many, including some councillors debating planning applications, as 'waste' which could be put to better use, such as industrial units.

I wrote many times about efforts to encourage the return of the distinctive red-billed chough, a playful member of the crow family, which had once been common in the county, and features on its coat of arms. This was an environmental issue close to Cornish hearts. There were many attempts, including the restoration of the coastal short grass the species needs, as well as captive breeding programmes, but in the end the birds made their own decisions. A small group of choughs just showed up in 2001, almost certainly from Ireland. They stayed and bred, perhaps joined by other incomers, and the Cornish chough population is now said to be about two hundred. Years after leaving Cornwall, I went back to Penwith and was thrilled to see them playing in the air above the coastal grassland.

I researched what was behind the disturbing number of dolphin carcasses washing up on beaches in Cornwall and in France. Many were mutilated, with fins missing, apparently having been hacked off. I spoke to a man who had been on a trawler and had seen dead dolphins caught in the netting as it was pulled back aboard. It seemed the poor creatures were the unfortunate victims of this method of fishing, caught and drowned in the nets, then hacked apart to get rid of them.

One day, just before moving into my cheap and tiny new home on the edge of the former mining village of St Day, near Redruth, which I had been lucky to buy before prices started rising, I was shifting a washing machine when something popped in my back, leaving me in terrible pain. As well as a clenched lower back, I had excruciating pain down my leg, which got worse the longer I was on my feet. I was told I had sciatica, caused by pressure on the sciatic nerve, probably from damage to one of the vertebral discs in my spine. My doctor prescribed painkillers. I couldn't stand long enough to have a shower without pain. There would be no more proper walking for almost eighteen months.

After a few weeks, despite still being in awful pain, I had to go back to work. It was a struggle. I couldn't afford to pay to park all day near the office, so had to walk in from the edge of Truro, finding window ledges and other unlikely places to sit for a few minutes when the pain became unbearable. The longer I remained upright, the more it hurt. Shopping in the supermarket, I'd have to crouch down and pretend to look for something on the lower shelves to ease the pain enough to get round the aisles and out. This horrendous sciatica lasted for more than a year. I couldn't walk for more than a few minutes without pain.

Life became difficult. I became depressed. I turned to drugs. I smoked cannabis every evening and all weekend. At first this eased my problems and the pain a little, but soon enough it began making them worse: it changed nothing in my life for the better and removed any drive I might have had to improve my circumstances. I went to the doctor, seeking some kind of counselling, but was put on anti-depressants, which made me feel terrible and made it hard to sleep. Of course, I had no way of knowing whether I'd be feeling even worse if I stopped taking them. The doctor advised me to continue. Then I was given different anti-depressants. Again I was told I needed to wait for them to work as it could take months. I still felt terrible, if not worse. I slid into feeling completely hopeless and having very dark thoughts. I went to work mostly, but felt like a zombie. I couldn't relate to the people around me at all. I disliked myself and almost everybody else.

I didn't see a doctor for months and months, until I made an appointment and happened to see a locum, who expressed surprise I hadn't been seen for so long. He referred me to a psychiatric nurse, who agreed I should slowly stop taking the drugs. He helped me find practical ways to feel better, and to gradually dig my way up through the layers of problems, until I could start to emerge into the world as me again. I have no idea how I managed to keep my job through it all. Years later I read that the particular drugs I had been prescribed for depression could also, in a small number of people, cause suicidal thoughts.

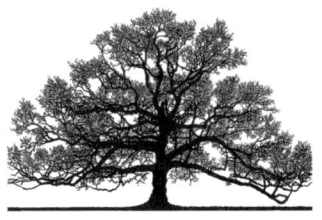

Love and Printmaking

Finding my kind and handsome partner Andrew changed my life. He was the nicest man I had ever met. He gave me love and stability, and thanks to him I gained financial security and was able to work part-time, then freelance. Without him I would never have discovered printmaking.

We met after he answered my entry in the Lonely Hearts column in The Guardian, years before online dating became normalised. Two 'relationship sought' ads I had placed in the gay press resulted in a flurry of nude photos from men primarily wanting sex, but two female friends had met partners via ads in The Guardian, so I thought I would give it a go. The ad appeared in print and respondents phoned a number and left a message, which I could listen to. I had twelve messages and Andrew's was the friendliest. We spoke on the phone a few times, then he came to Cornwall to see me. It seems bizarre now, but at that point we hadn't even seen photos of each other. It was a strange start to a relationship, but somehow we worked it out.

After a while, we decided to live together and moved to Devon. I got a job on another paper. For six months we rented a holiday cottage on Exmoor, where we walked the moors and the wooded river valleys.

It was such a different landscape from Cornwall. There were so many trees and the woods were large. Cornwall had beautiful estuaries, but inland rivers were not so impressive. On Exmoor we lived near the River Barle, a clean and beautiful river whose banks were rich with oaks and beeches. On a sunny day in autumn the Barle glowed with the deep gold beech leaves lining its bed and floating on its water. We often heard the stags roaring in the rutting season. I discovered Horner Wood, an 800-acre ancient oak wood on the National Trust's Holnicote Estate. It was the biggest wood I had encountered since walking in the New Forest.

One weekend I drove north to where the most extensive sections of unbroken moorland remain and started on a walk which should have taken me a few hours. It had been a while since I had needed to carefully read a map, as in Cornwall I knew my way around so well, and on Exmoor we had, so far, stuck mostly to river walks, where direction finding is easier. Part-way through I realised the landscape features didn't match where I thought I was on the map. I was lost, in a way I had never experienced before. The landscape was almost devoid of features, just gently rolling moorland to the horizon. One part looked very much like another, and with no fixed points: no walls, rivers or buildings. I just couldn't work out where I actually was. I didn't even own a mobile phone, and realised I should have brought a compass. I kept walking, following a direction based on the position of the sun, banking on reaching something discernible eventually. It was warm. I used up my water and became very thirsty. My boots were newish and started to hurt. The small rises and descents went on and on. An hour later, my feet were so painful I didn't dare take off my boots to look. I found a drinking trough for sheep, fed by a pipe coming from who knows where. I didn't care. I drank from it and filled my water bottle. I eventually found a wall and made a best guess as to where I might be in relation to the map. I followed the wall and finally found a road which allowed me to navigate back to my car. The next day I had an enormous blister on my heel, which soon turned into an alarming hole. I limped for weeks.

We bought a house in a village called Lapford, just below the border between Mid and North Devon. I worked on the local paper in Barnstaple, before moving to another paper in Tiverton. After a few years there we moved to the south of the county, to a four-storey house in a valley surrounded by woods, with the moors of Dartmoor a mile up the hill. On the top floor, with a little imagination, I felt like I was in the trees.

I only knew what printmaking was as the result of a visit to linocut printmaker Elizabeth Rashleigh in Newton Abbot, during an open studios event. She was kind enough to explain how she went from drawing to carving to print. I realised we had bought a print in a gallery in St Ives, 'Bathing Lovers' by the wonderful printmaker Trevor Price, without even knowing it was one. A couple of months later my neighbour told me, over the fence, that she was about to start attending a printmaking workshop at Dartington, near Totnes, once a week. Why didn't I give it a go?

At the time Andrew had a proper job and I had less work than usual, so had more free time, and winter was approaching. I remembered the linocut artist and how intrigued I had been when she showed me how she used her beautiful Victorian printing press. I arranged to visit the Dartington Print Workshop, where I met the man who had been running it for more than thirty years. Michael Honnor, I later learned, was committed to it being run as an educational workshop, open to beginners and professional artists alike.

I told him I had no art education, no practical experience of drawing or painting or anything, and would need lots of help. Perhaps to give me courage, he rummaged beneath a table, pulled out a box filled with books and picked one up. It was, I discovered afterwards, A Printmakers' Flora, a huge and stunning handmade book of prints of British wild flowers made by members of the workshop.

As I turned the pages, Michael mentioned the names of the printmakers who had contributed to it. One had been a member for decades, some had attended for a few years, while, if I remember rightly, another was new to printmaking.

It was beyond my imagination that a new workshop member could make a print that would be included in such a beautiful book. My jaw dropped further when Michael told me that one of the few copies offered for sale had just been bought by Yale University, for its Center for British Art, for a large sum of money. 'Come next week and bring a drawing,' he said.

I didn't set out to make prints of trees, let alone to sell my prints. I just wanted to have a go and hopefully be able to make something. It was really hard. Learning from scratch was not easy in a workshop where I struggled alongside excellent printmakers, some of whom were professional artists and most of whom had been to art school. I felt very exposed. They could all see my failures. It gave me a weekly migraine, and I wasn't an easy student. I found the vulnerability of not knowing what to do next very difficult. Printmaking is a craft and there is a lot of process. It takes quite a while to get to grips with, and remember, all the different stages, and you need to know them all before you can start to progress on your own. The biggest drawback for a learner – but also the biggest benefit – was that the workshop was not a course. There were beginners, but each person was taught more or less individually. This was wonderful because I received tuition to suit my level of skills and what I wanted to make, and could learn from the work of the printmakers around me, but difficult because they also wanted Michael's help.

On my first day Michael sat me opposite the other new beginner that term. Henry was working on a very interesting wooded landscape. He didn't look much like a beginner to me. As we chatted we got on to the subject of trees. He told me he was working in his studio at home on a project involving a tree. He had cut it down, then sawn it up into small sections. Now he was reassembling it as a kind of sculpture. He showed me a photo. Sitting in the middle of a large and stunningly white space, was an entire tree, in bits. The room was his studio. He might have been a beginner printmaker, but he certainly wasn't new to art and creativity. Henry turned out to be the artist behind two projects which had caught attention and delighted the public. The first was a 20-foot-tall wooden chair, which he had erected in a field above Widecombe in the Moor on Dartmoor. People went to see it in their hundreds and thousands, so many that the National Park Authority said they were causing traffic problems and issued an enforcement notice to have the chair removed. After that, Henry made a huge ladder, which narrowed towards the top, making it look even taller. It was a big attraction too, but was sadly felled by a storm.

Michael was much in demand. He couldn't spend the whole day with me; he would guide me through to the next stage, but then I'd lose him and be left with no clue as to what to do next. I fantasised about attaching an elasticated lead to his waist, so I could yank him back when I needed him. He was patient, helpful and wise, but sometimes he overestimated how much I knew. When I was ready to print my first plate, he showed me the paper preparation area and left me with the instruction, 'Prepare your paper'. I had no idea what that involved. Prepare it how? Make it? He meant trim it to the size I wanted, either by cutting it for a smooth edge or tearing it to give rough edges, but I didn't know how large it needed to be or how to tear paper so the edge was both rough and straight. I didn't know how to tear paper full stop.

While I was waiting for Michael to come back, I had the opportunity to look at what everyone else was doing. As the weeks went by I also realised how amazing it was to see ten or twelve different people, who mostly all attended on the same day each week, move their ideas from thought to ink to paper. There were large communal drying racks: metal structures with lift-up grids on which prints sat drying. Looking through them was a delight. Each week I could see not only the progress made by the people who attended on my day, but also of those who attended on other days. As I got to know the people, and their prints, I found I could recognise who had made a particular new print. Everyone had a style, or look, that was surprisingly easy to identify.

I had no drawing skills, no idea of colours or how to mix them, but I was absolutely determined to keep going. I sensed printmaking was my way into art, craft and the world of making things. It seemed more accessible for a beginner than other art-related activities I had tried.

It wasn't long before I made my first proper print. Scratching away at a bit of plastic with an old nail I'd been given by Michael, I attempted to transfer the lines of a drawing of a pine tree

Love and Printmaking

I'd seen while walking on Dartmoor. When all the lines were scratched, I was shown how to ink it, then how to put it through the press. As it came out, I lifted the paper and hey presto, there was an image.

It wasn't great, but somehow, through the process of scratching lines, inking them and wiping the surface clean, my rubbish drawing had been transformed into something that looked like something. I don't mean it looked like the tree that inspired it, or that it was any good, but that it had gained a character, a look or a quality that elevated it above the drawing I'd struggled with. Without trying, I sort of had a style. Perhaps, I thought, I could make pleasing prints even if I couldn't draw.

As I progressed I tried different printmaking techniques. The pine, and a few other early prints, were drypoints, a method of scratching lines into plastic, then pushing ink into them and wiping the surface clean. Like drawing, it printed the lines I drew. After that I moved on to relief printmaking, using vinyl flooring rather than lino. The task was to draw an image on it, then carve away the background to leave the drawing in relief, ready to have ink rolled on the surface.

I dabbled with etching, scratching lines into copper then dunking them in acid to etch them deeper, and with collagraphs, a mysterious process of gluing materials on to a flat surface. Different materials held or rejected ink differently. Some held ink well, so would make a solid area of colour when printed, while the ink slid off others, meaning that area would be lighter, or even white. This was all really interesting, but I kept coming back to relief printmaking. I tried making images with many colours using a relief process called reduction, but found it went wrong too often. Days of work and lots of expensive printmaking paper went to waste if you made a slight misjudgement, because you could never properly go back. The plate you printed from was carved away bit by bit for each layer of colour, until there was virtually nothing left of it. One mistake usually meant disaster. I was still learning and should have been kinder to myself, but I really wanted to make something that looked good. I became so fed up with one reduction attempt, I chucked the plate and all the prints in the bin, to the horror of those around me.

I knew I was enjoying the carving part of the relief printmaking process. It was slow and gentle and engaged only part of my brain, leaving the rest to wander – a bit like walking. After drawing my image on the vinyl flooring, I would slowly carve around it, removing the surface colour and cutting through to an off-white layer below, which beautifully showed up the black pen drawing I was carving around. It was so satisfying to spend an evening working on it, then see how much more of the image had been revealed in stark relief.

I bought some carving tools of my own and started doing the carving at home. I became quite engrossed in it, spending much of my free time working on something related to printmaking, even printing plates by hand using wooden spoons to burnish the back of the paper and get the ink to transfer on to it.

Many printmakers radically simplify the images they want to translate into print, sometimes giving the print a flat look, almost like a cartoon drawing. I tried this, but didn't like it. Instead, I started to get more complex, which didn't work for me either, especially given my inexperience. I made a complicated reduction print of a Devon landscape: the view from Raddon Hill north of Exeter, which is topped by a solitary and majestic pine. After I'd carved the dozens of complex fields and colours fading into distant purples and greys, I was left with the tree. Depicting all the shades of green and grey within it felt beyond me, so I decided to just leave it as a green silhouette. I don't think it worked that well, but it left a seed in my mind.

A while later my friend Olwen was showing me some of her photographs when one caught my eye. It was of a branch and tree with the moon behind. Like all her photos, it was beautiful and the colours were amazing. I drew it out in a simplified silhouette, but left as much of the complexity of the tree and the branch as I could. I carved it. It was very slow work. It took days and days. I could hardly wait to get into the workshop to print it. When I did, I was entranced by it.

The 'reveal' moment in printmaking is something quite extraordinary. Through the carving process you don't really know what it's going to look like, not least because the image will be in reverse. I don't make any proof prints during the carving, as I fear the necessary inking, then cleaning, will erase the lines I've taken days to draw. So I wait until I've finished carving to ink the plate, put paper on top and put it through the press. When it comes out the other side, and the paper is pulled gently away from the press, it is the first time I have seen it. It's quite a moment, particularly when a plate has taken a month to carve. When you're new to printmaking, it is especially magical.

This branch, tree and moon print felt new and interestingly complex, but also simple as it was all printed in black. Next I tried adding a background colour by cutting another piece of the vinyl flooring the same size, removing a small circle to remain as a white moon. I think I printed it in a kind of misty pinkish colour. Then I printed the tree and branch on top. Now I had complexity and simplicity, as well as colour and, most important for me, I had something I was pleased with. I had also found a way to make an image which was repeatable. I could change the background colour as much as I liked because the component plates – the tree and the background – were still intact. A few of my fellow printmakers made encouraging remarks, and for the first time, I felt as if I'd made something interesting. I was eager to make another.

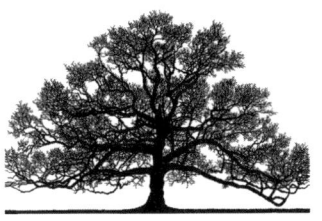

Rain

I knew the west of Britain was wetter than London and the east because I grew up on a western coast battered by gales and rain, but when I moved from London to Cornwall it seemed to rain even more than I remembered. My first autumn there, it rained every day for months. The continual rain was noteworthy – the Western Morning News went as far as to keep a daily tally on its front page. At one point I went to see my parents in Wales and, as the train passed through the Somerset Levels on a raised embankment, it was like travelling across a vast lake.

My home in Cornwall was on the high ground in the middle of the west of the county, and, later, in south Devon, I lived just below the moors. Both locations were on an almost continuous spine of cloud-and-rain-attracting hills running from the tip of Cornwall through the Cornish clay country, to Bodmin Moor, then Dartmoor. It can be wet or misty on these hills, but dry and sunny a few miles nearer the coast. One early spring day in Cornwall,

I walked with friends in a cold drizzle on the Penwith moors, wearing warm clothes and full waterproofs, while just a few miles away, on a beach in a bay near Porthcurno, a friend was tanning himself on the sand.

I had to make an accommodation with the rain. There was no point hating it. There was nothing I could do to stop it. I had to find ways to change how I felt about it. I bought better boots and waterproof trousers and tried to think positively about it.

A little later in my life I used positive thought in a similar way when I tried to make peace with a different negative at our house in south Devon. We had previously lived in the middle of a village and had been bothered by the noise of the many boy racers roaring up and down the main street. Our new house was a mile from the small town of Ashburton, on a single-track road with passing places. Before we bought it we visited at different times of day and it seemed quiet, but when we moved in we were disappointed to discover we could hear the regular whoosh of passing cars. We mentioned this to the first few friends who came to stay. They would look at us quizzically: we'd all listen for a bit, hear nothing, then we'd realise it was a ridiculous thing to say to anyone used to life in a large town or city. Here there were too few cars for them to even notice. They laughed at us. But, I still resented the cars I heard, until I decided not to. I made an effort to imagine the cars being driven by friendly and interesting people on their way somewhere nice, to see a friend perhaps. Somehow this worked. After a while I no longer noticed the infrequent passing traffic.

On a winter walk through the Cornwall Wildlife Trust nature reserve at Ponsanooth, near Falmouth, I couldn't fail to notice the pouring rain. I remembered the power of the water on my ill-fated attempt to climb Cadair Idris in Wales. I tried again to let myself enjoy its drama. Water was the whole reason behind what had happened in Kennall Vale, a manufacturing site for gunpower used in mining and quarrying in the nineteenth century. Waterwheels were used to power the manufacturing processes in buildings which still stand in the now-wooded valley. The water came from the wild and boulder-strewn river via leats, channels built to guide the water from further up the river to the waterwheels.

I went there after a night of heavy rain, in a week when it had rained every day. Water was everywhere, crashing down the river and overspilling the leats. It felt like it was coming at me from every angle. I had never been anywhere quite like it: powerful, noisy, magnificent, on the edge of being out of control ... and all about the rain and the water.

Without the rain, the beautiful wet woods around the edges of Dartmoor would not be the same. More than a metre of rain a year is needed to sustain our native temperate rainforests, championed so passionately by Guy Shrubsole in The Lost Rainforests of Britain. The highest parts of Dartmoor may get over 2,000 mm of rain per year and the southern edges might receive 1,000 mm, while London averages just 500 to 600 mm per year.

Only fragments of British rainforest are left: in Scotland, the Lake District, Wales, Devon and Cornwall. They are places rich with a special mix of ferns, fungi, lichens and mosses, growing not only on the ground, but also on rocks and on the trees themselves. Living on the edge of Dartmoor I was lucky enough to have plenty to visit. Shaptor Woods, which sits high above the town of Bovey Tracey and the Wray Valley, is one of the best.

On a day of showers after a late November night of heavy rain, I set out to visit Shaptor. I reached it via the beautifully named Bearacleave Wood, where a line of huge beeches grows from the remains of a Devon hedgebank, broken limbs scattered in the undergrowth like the remains of giant statues. I walked along the rusty carpet of their leaves and the distinctive saw-toothed ones from an old sweet chestnut, as water suddenly cascaded from the trees in a gust. I followed the bank down a steep slope to a green lane. This was also lined with beeches and littered with enormous cross-sections of those which had fallen across it and been cleared by chainsaw. One big chunk faced me cut-side-on, a log for a giant's hearth, the wood too wet and dark to count the rings, the width of the trunk greater than the length of my arm. I went through the gate into Shaptor, picking my way across little streams, where it is dry in summer, to a pair of beeches flanking the path. They were so large it would have taken three of me to hug them. On the north side the trunks were green and thick with moss, on the south they were grey with lichen in patches and patterns.

I walked on into an increasingly green and messy place, a mix of all sorts, including what looked like the multiple stems of coppiced hazel and the odd, larger oak. There must be dormice here, I thought. I looked for hazelnut shells, hoping to find the distinctive tooth-mark pattern on the outside edge of a smooth hole in the shell, but found nothing. Too late in the season. They had probably rotted away. Ivy grew up most of the oaks, then trailed down into the air on ropes I could have caught, but not climbed. On one old oak the ivy stems were as thick as my arm.

A glimpse of sun illuminated the diamond raindrops still hanging from the ends of every delicate twig. It started to rain again. I was snug in my coat and waterproof trousers. I began to spot the big, round-edged boulders which make this wood so distinctive, these ones like resting creatures, covered with moss and ferns: camouflage they might shake off in an instant and rise up in front of me in their granite glory. On a higher patch there were huge, smooth rocks in whose mossy fur grew patches of round-leaved pennywort and the remains of their tall flowers. The pattern of leaves looked like a hundred ripples in a pond. Trees grew from the gaps between the boulders. Small and twisted oaks looked older than their size would suggest. Perhaps their roots were restricted by the granite: a natural bonsai. I climbed up on to the tor, where the height and the arrangement of boulders made it feel more like the remains of a building, a small fort in a watery kingdom.

I crossed more streams on plank bridges, some of which were now surrounded by water on both sides. I jumped the flood to firmer ground. Below the water, the soil had been washed away to reveal sand and granite grit, cream and gold in colour. The lightness was startling in this place of darker tones on a day without sun. I spotted an invasive laurel seedling and pulled it up. The path started to climb steeply. The trees around were mostly leafless, but their trunks were still wrapped in a thick coat of ivy. I startled a buzzard, which shot off noisily. I passed an old and dying ash, another victim of ash dieback.

I came to what looked like the remains of a wall, at right angles to the path. A line of bigger oaks roughly followed it. I could imagine this wood might once have been a pasture studded with trees, with more marking the boundaries. Enormous fallen trunks and branches lay where they had landed and were now home to gardens in the air, the decaying wood hosting carpets of moss and ferns. I felt like an explorer in a place nature had so thoroughly taken over. I remembered reading about the Amazon and how parts of what is now seen as pristine jungle were once densely populated. Many of the inhabitants are thought to have died from imported European diseases, probably long before the Spanish colonisers even reached them, and the jungle returned, a testament to the power of the natural world. Sometimes, all it needs is to be left alone.

This is what seems to have happened at Shaptor, where several sections of ancient woodland were once separated by fields which, presumably, stopped being used to graze animals at some point. Once the grazing was limited, the fields began reverting to woodland, joining it all together again.

I passed a huge oak, which had fallen, but not died. The larger branches had sent up vertical shoots, some now a foot in diameter. On a stool of rotting wood I saw a patch of dark green moss, each stem growing straight up, looking like a miniature pine forest. The rotting remains of the trunk next to it sprouted toadstools: everything constantly being recycled.

I crossed a bigger stream into a clearing full of what appeared to be sycamore saplings, then another line of oaks presumably marking an old field boundary. I was brought to a halt by two fallen trees. They must have been growing right next to each other. When one fell, the other toppled too, but in the other direction. Now they lay like a mirror image of each other, stump to stump, flanking a hole in the ground like the entrance to an underground world. I stepped down into it, seeing holes within the hole, imagining they led deeper still to some creature's subterranean lair. I moved on, stooping to get under one of the trunks. I saw a southern wood ants' nest, an impressive mound of twigs and debris 2 feet tall. In spring and summer the surface would be seething with ants. Now it seemed still and I put my hand on it. As soon as I did so, the surface moved. I quickly took my hand away. These must be guard ants, slowed by the cold, but still ready to defend their home by showering me with formic acid.

I reached my favourite part of the wood, a collection of gargantuan boulders, some lying on top of others, hundreds of tons of granite rock propped up by the same. Already in a Victorian explorer frame of mind, I couldn't help but imagine them as the remains of a temple. The boulders seemed to have rounded edges, like pebbles on a beach. Up close the granite was rougher than I had imagined and studded with quartz. The closer I looked the more there was to see. A whole world of rifts and rocky shelves opened up. The ledges, which looked like green lines from afar, were full of plants growing in the water they held. The surface of the rock was much more complex than was evident from a distance. The composite minerals, as well as the different mosses and powdery grey lichen, made a subtle mosaic in a palette of greys, pinks and greens.

Throughout the wood was evidence of the wind the night before: lichen-covered twigs blown off the trees, now lying on the paths, their luminous green-blue-grey the palest thing in sight.

I saw a laurel and went to pull it up, but it was too big. There were more huge oaks, many with large growths, probably burr knots, which are the result of stress, for example if animals are grazing their lower parts. The loss causes dormant buds under the bark to grow, bursting through a bit wildly, forming rough-textured large bumps. I wondered if maybe these were formed long ago, when the trees were standing in a pasture and were grazed by livestock.

While looking at them I felt something brush my neck and immediately thought of jumping spiders. I remembered when, walking in Boro Wood behind my home one morning the previous autumn, I had encountered this kind of spider for the first time. I'd felt something on my neck and caught it in my hand. It was a spider, but one with a longer and less-rounded shape than more familiar spiders. The head and body were roughly the same size, rather than the bigger body/smaller head common on the kinds of spiders I was used to. Almost immediately I felt something else on my neck, which I quickly brushed away. That evening, I felt something move under my shirt and was horrified to discover it was the jumping spider I thought I had removed. Horribly, it had been inside my clothes the whole day. Thankfully, in Shaptor Woods the neck-brusher turned out to be just a hanging tendril of ivy.

As I walked on I realised I'd lost the path. At the same moment the rain came beating down. I pushed through a patch of holly for shelter, hoping the path was a little lower down – and it was. I reached two rounded boulders resting upright on a ledge on a slope, with a tiny gap between them. They looked like a sculpture. Barbara Hepworth sprang to mind: both the sculptures in the garden of her studio and the rock forms and standing stones on the Penwith moors in Cornwall, from which she took inspiration.

As I neared the end of the path I noticed how large some of the ferns had become. Some had the appearance of miniature tree ferns, with trunks, albeit short ones. Over the years new fronds had grown above the remains of those withered by the previous winter, giving them a height and exotic stature. Looking ahead, I saw a fallen oak, caught by those around it and held at an angle. I followed the path as it climbed steeply again, up towards Shaptor Down, giving me views west towards the moors. I decided to turn back, saving whatever there was to see up there until next time.

Earlier, when we lived north of the moor, my favourite place was a valley in which grew Black-a-tor Copse, one of the three tiny remnants of the ancient upland oak forest which is thought to have once covered most of Dartmoor. The best known of these is Wistman's Wood, further south, on the banks of the West Dart river. Wistman's is not that far from a road, so is quite accessible. Black-a-tor, which runs along the bank of the West Okement river, is a bit of a walk to get to, but worth it, as it is just as enchanting a place and a little larger. The trees in both are stunted, twisted and hanging with ferns and lichens, growing among mossy boulders. It is probably the boulders which saved both of the woods. Both sites are grazed by sheep – which love to munch on oak seedlings – but the boulders keep them out to some extent. Any acorn which manages to grow outside the boulder field is not likely to survive.

Years ago, when I was writing an opinion column for newspapers in Devon (which I did under a pseudonym for fourteen years), I wrote a piece about Wistman's, trying to draw attention to the disparity between its high profile as a wonderful, romantic and important place, and the fact that not much appeared to be happening to ensure its future or expand it. All that seemed to be needed was the exclusion of sheep from the wood itself and, hopefully, from a larger area around it, into which the oaks could seed. So, I was delighted to hear last year that a tiny piece of the thousands and thousands of acres of sheep grazing on Dartmoor was to be protected around the wood boundary, so it could spread. I don't know whether sheep have yet been excluded from Black-a-tor Copse, but they hadn't the last time I visited it.

To reach it, I started at Meldon Reservoir, where one sunny day in early autumn I witnessed uncountable numbers of swallows and house martins pausing their migration to drink from the water. There were so many, and they were so quick, that when I looked at the water I couldn't distinguish one from the other, seeing instead a constant rippling of the surface as they dipped and touched it, as if a giant bucket of gravel was continually being cast across it.

At my house in south Devon I also once saw part of the great southerly movement of swallows. Looking out the window one day I noticed that there were far more swallows in the air than usual. I went outside and looked up and around. The sky was full of them, but when I turned to look at the house, I saw an astonishing sight.

The entire four-storey façade was covered with birds, clinging on to the render, chattering loudly and jumping off to fly around and feed, then landing back on it.

The last time I went to Meldon, then on to Black-a-tor, it was the middle of winter: a day of dramatic skies and fierce showers. As I left the reservoir behind I descended into a marshy area, then followed the river upstream. Around the side of Homerton Hill I entered the valley of the West Okement. On the western side the moor rose like a cliff. On the other there was a similarly steep climb up to Black Tor, whose rocky outcrops could be seen from below. The whole valley was thickly littered with rocks, or clitter, as it is called on Dartmoor. The section of the map for that valley, and the slopes around it, is so densely covered with tiny circular shapes to depict the rocky debris, it looks as if someone started drawing them and couldn't stop.

There were plenty of people walking near the reservoir, but none to be seen here. As I walked on I came to a strangely dense area of trees, unlike anything you ever see on the moor. As I got closer I saw the trees were inside a wall, which had been built in a rectangular shape, with the river bisecting it. I wondered whether it had been, originally, a small reservoir. Ironically, it sits within sight of Black-a-tor. The irony being that the only reason there was such dense growth of pioneer trees inside these walls is because they exclude the sheep, while just up the valley was an important, but unprotected, historic wood.

The path led up the valley to the copse, its trees similar to those at Wistman's in their contorted forms and low height, but generally not as dense. I sat on a boulder to eat my sandwich, listening to the roar of the river as it crashed against the boulders. I felt fairly safe to do so, as it was winter. In spring and summer I knew better than to linger in a spot like that. Once in summer I had sat nearby on a

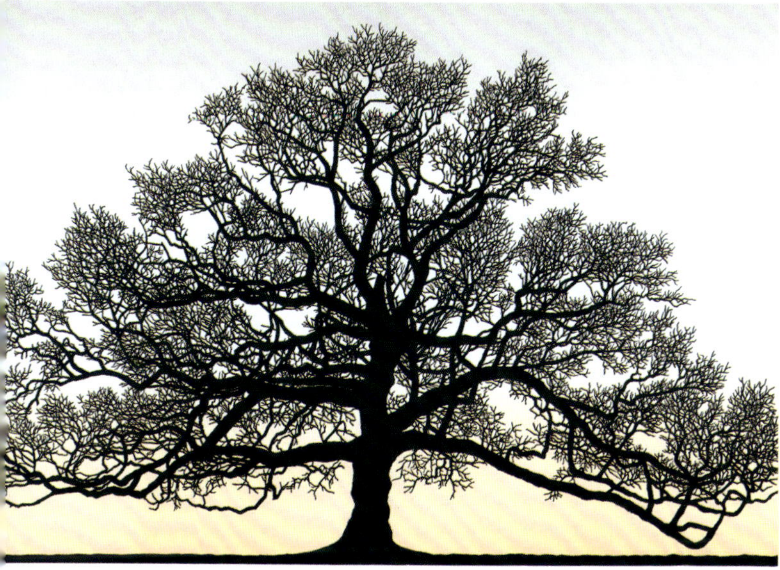

I Have Lived a Thousand Storms

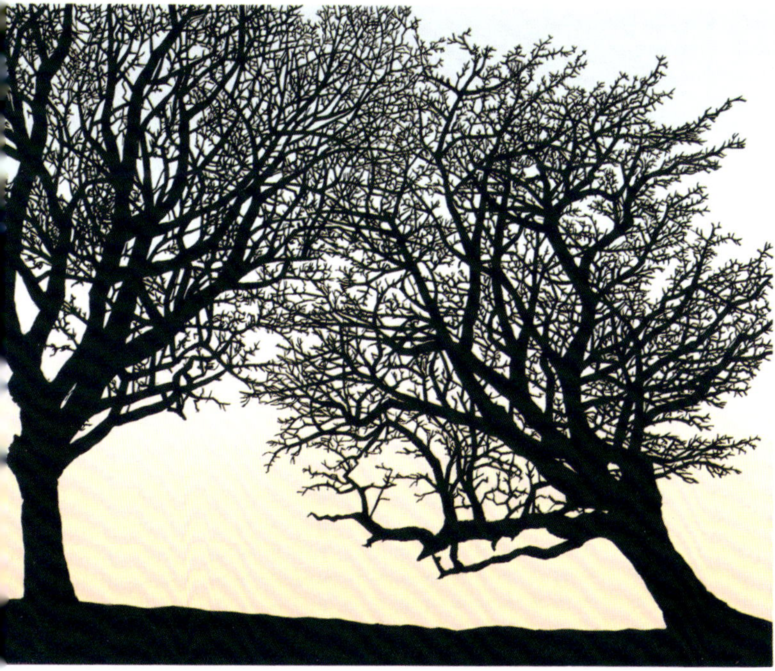

Balance

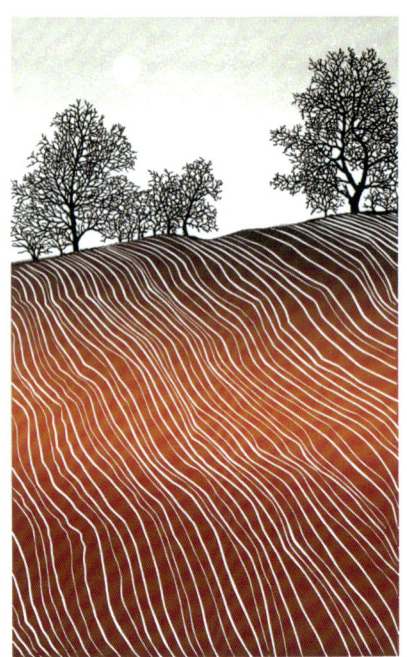
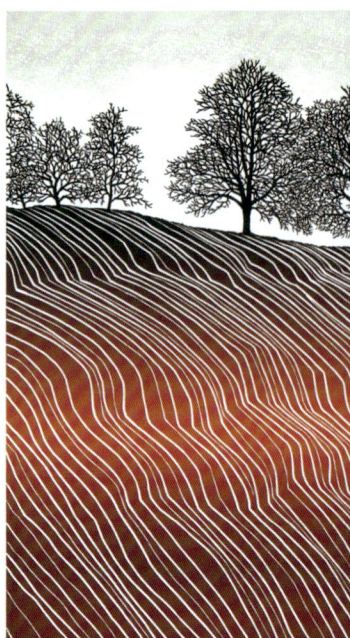

Big Field I & II

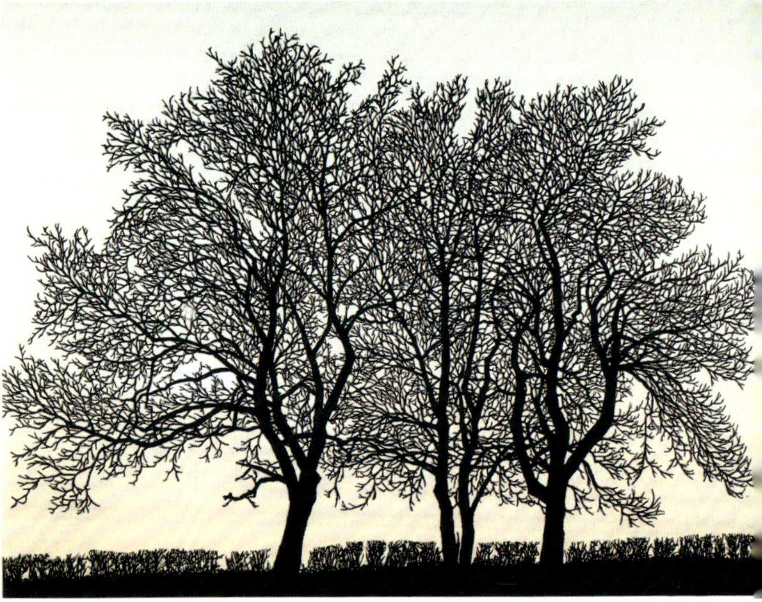

Last to Leaf First to Fall

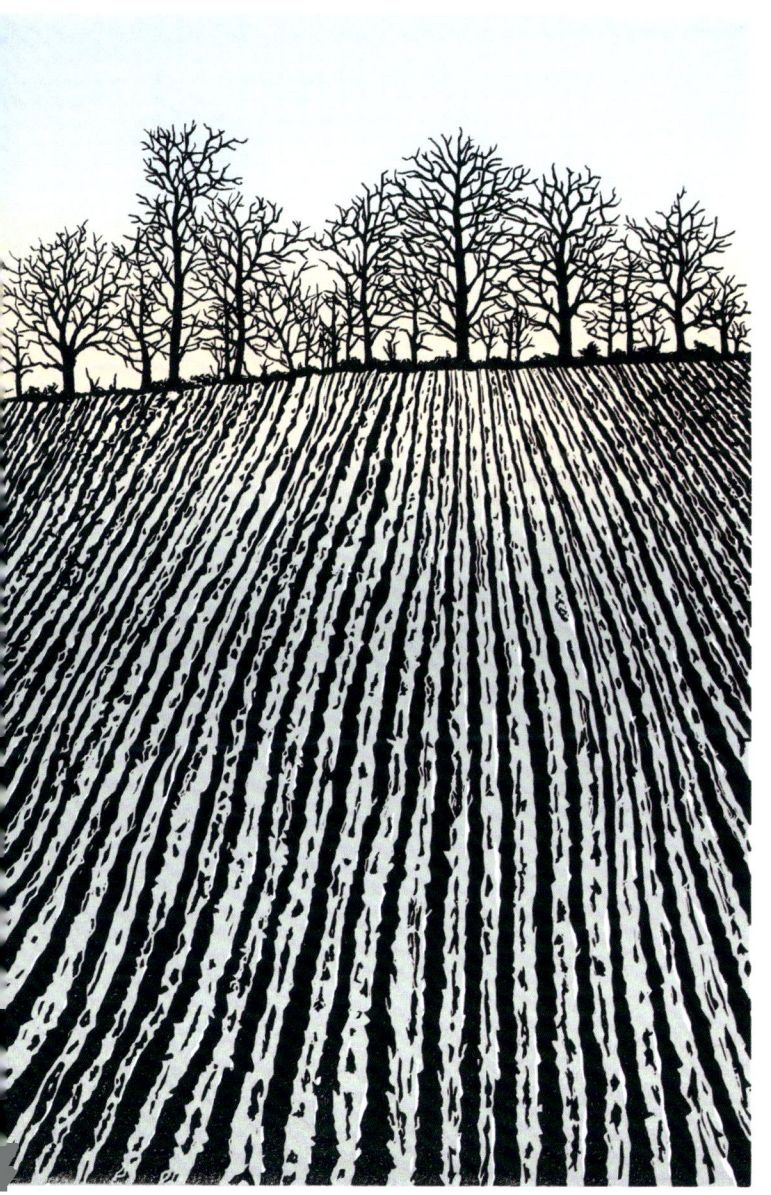
Ploughed Field

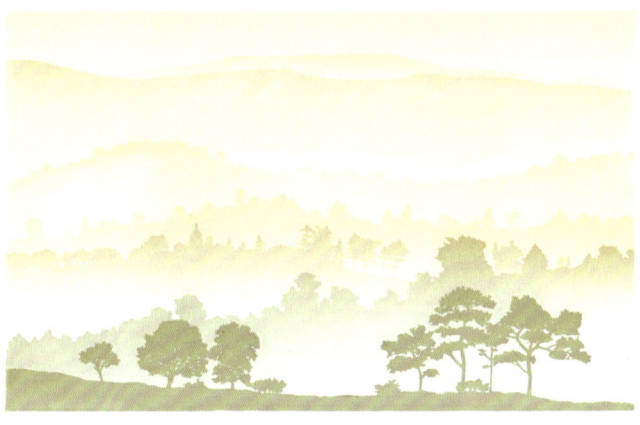

East of the Moor

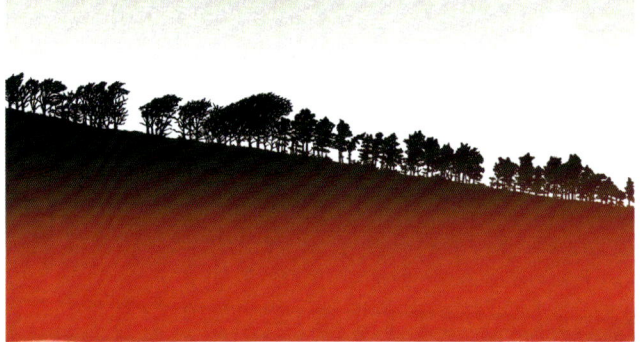

Ridge

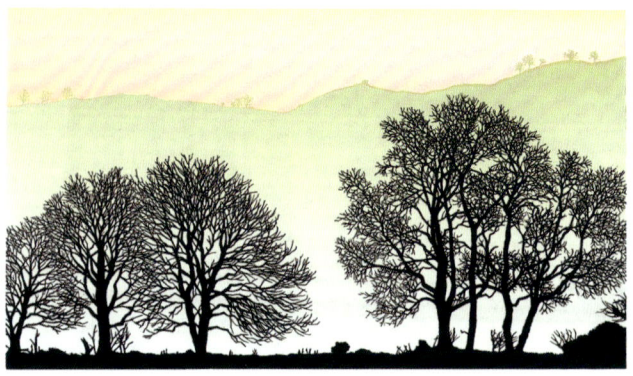

In the Valley

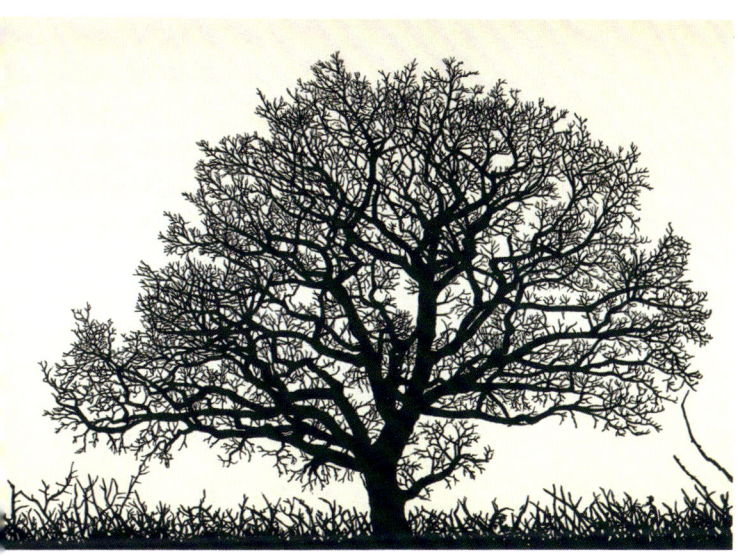

Hedge Oak

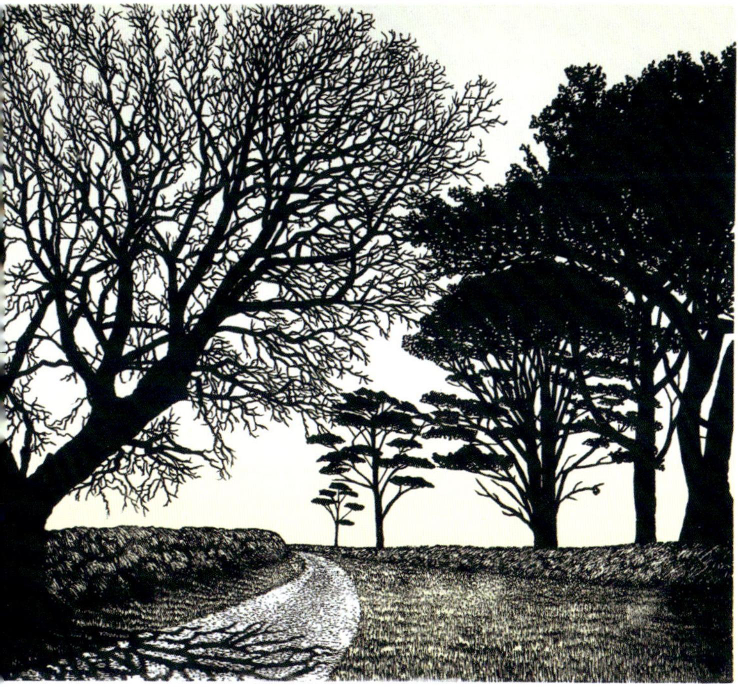

To the Sea

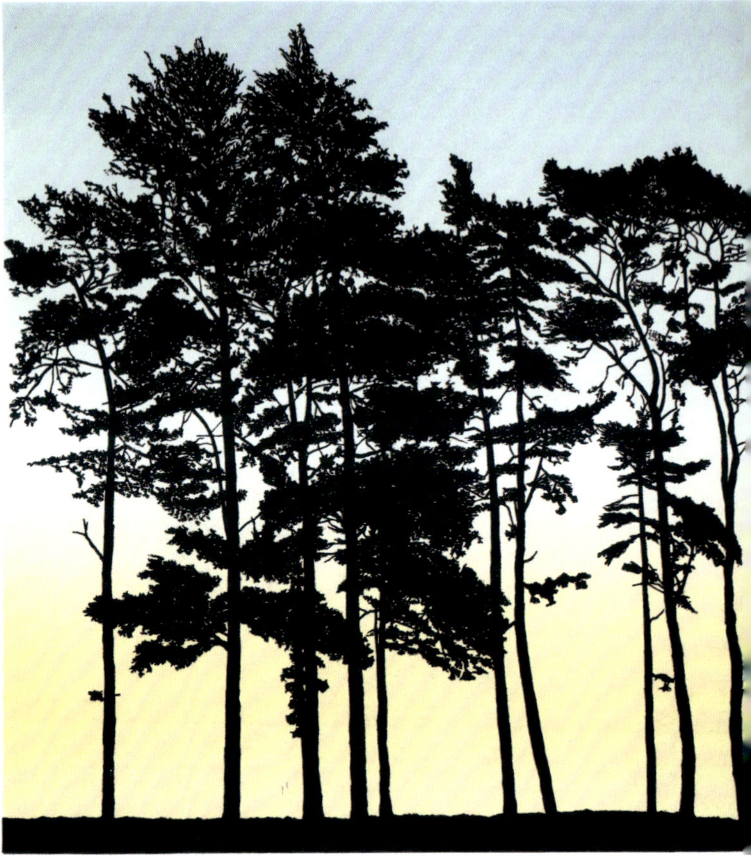

The Sentinels

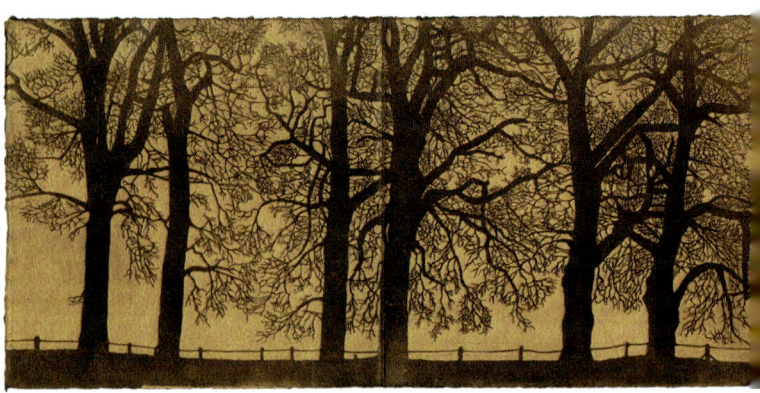

Grey Black Trees on Gold

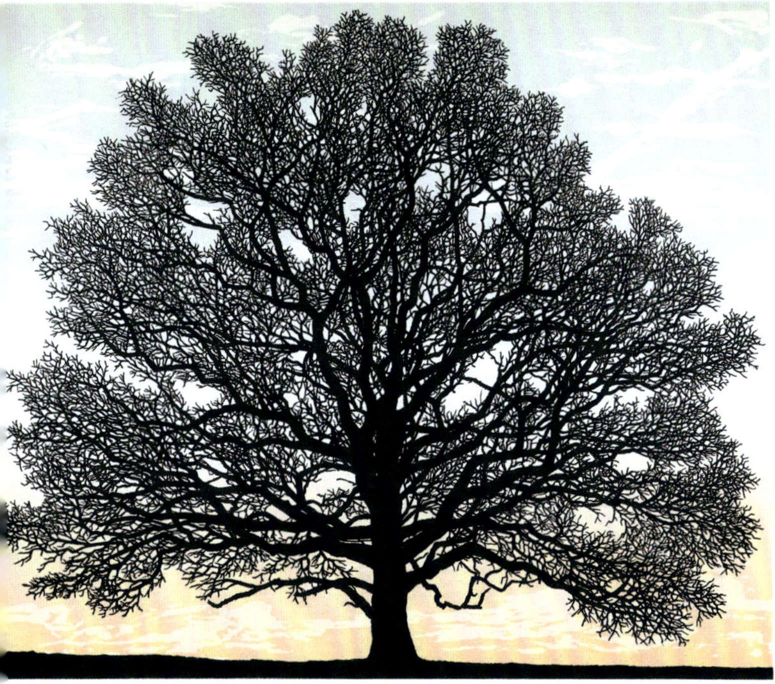

Dartmoor Oak

Follow the River

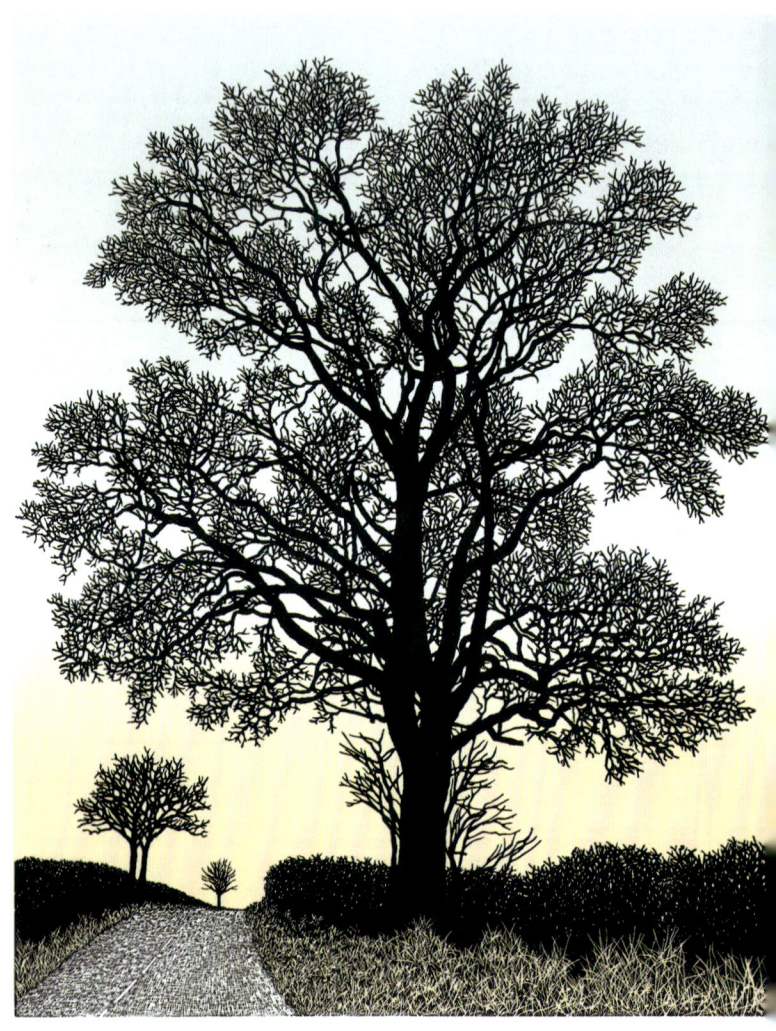

Road Home

Rain

sunny day, in a comfortable hollow between the rocks, and started to read. I was wearing shorts and hadn't been living in Devon long. I felt an itch on my leg and, looking down, saw that it was covered with dozens of tiny insects. They were ticks. Not just the one or two you might see on your trousers after walking through grass or bracken in other parts of the moor, but dozens, and tiny, presumably newly hatched, alerted to my presence by my movement and the carbon dioxide I was exhaling. They were probably seeking their first meal – me. I frantically picked them off. You can't brush them away as their legs have an amazing grip. You have to pick them off. Otherwise, they march up your legs until they find a patch of skin which takes their fancy. First they anaesthetise the area so you feel nothing, then they push their heads into your skin and start feeding on your blood. They are the scourge of walking on Dartmoor or, more accurately, of walking through undergrowth or sitting in the wrong place. Finding one feeding on you is unpleasant, to say the least, but they also carry various diseases, including Lyme Disease, which can be serious. I've been bitten by many ticks, but thankfully have never developed the symptomatic Lyme bullseye rash. I think that encounter at Black-a-tor was the last time I wore shorts on the moor. These days, in times of peak tick activity, I avoid certain areas, make sure not to push through dense undergrowth and always try to wear light-coloured trousers, so I can easily spot them and flick them off.

As printmaking started to take over my life, I also began to look at the south Devon landscape more closely. I'd always loved mist, fog and snow, and the way they change everything, softening the view and reducing distant trees and hills to pale silhouettes, but here I began to see rain differently. Sitting in my house on days of rain and wind, I loved how the dark background provided by the tree-covered hill opposite allowed me to see the airborne drifts of mist-coloured rain sweeping in front of it. I'd rarely experienced rain as something with such physical form before. This wasn't about seeing drops of rain, but whole murmurations of them, millions of raindrops given a fleeting form by the wind, driven across the valley in waves and shifting patterns. Yet, surprisingly, there were also patches of calm above the treetops in the lee of the wind, where the humid air was still enough for mist to form. I imagined raindrops shattering into minute fragments as they hit the trees, then staying airborne above them – like astronauts in a zero-gravity chamber – as the wind was diverted higher by the mass of the woods and the hill, hitting the exposed trees at the top, showering the woodland floor with debris.

Once, walking in a Dartmoor wood with friends, we experienced something extraordinary. Out of nowhere an immense wind suddenly hit us, so strong we could barely move forward and were trapped in a whirlwind of leaves and twigs. It lasted perhaps five minutes. It was calm as we drove home, but the roads were thick with twigs and branches. We had to go slowly and carefully.

When I moved to my peculiar four-storey house near Ashburton (known to most locally as the Coffin House, or Coffin Mill, because of its shape from above – tall and thin, coming to a point in the road, a miniature version of the Flat Iron building in New York), I went on a long walk most days, clocking up dozens of miles a week. That, combined with being six foot two in a world mostly designed for shorter people, and not paying enough attention to the height of the surfaces I was working on, led to another disc problem in my back. I was walking on the moor above the valley one day when I suddenly started to feel pain in my leg. The next day my back was clenched and standing was painful. Luckily this time I had a good doctor, who quickly referred me for a scan, which showed the disc had effectively burst, expelling much of its contents into the adjacent space, where some of it was pressing against the sciatic nerve. There would be no more walking for a while. It was devastating.

Months went by. I made the best of it, still printmaking, but very carefully and trying not to be on my feet too much. My friend Vincent made me a carving slope and I bought a more ergonomically designed chair. Now I could be reasonably comfortable and carve without any bending. The plate I was working on rested on the slope, which had both a lip at the bottom to hold it and an adjustable wooden band at the top so it didn't move as I pushed on it while I carved. I bought a magnifying lamp, which took a powerful daylight bulb and could be adjusted to sit the right distance above the plate. I started drawing and carving larger and more intricate trees, as I could do that sitting down and I had plenty of time. I based some on photos taken by Olwen and some by me. I became quite obsessive about it. The rest of life had become a bit difficult, but I felt productive and content if I was making something. I took the plates I carved at home to the workshop and printed them on the press there.

I was almost always in discomfort and sometimes in pain. I was progressed up the ladder of treatment: next was the steroid injection into my back. In the waiting room, I sat beside a grey-faced man who was sitting for the obligatory fifteen minutes after the injection, carefully sipping a cup of tea. I asked him whether the injection had hurt. He looked at me and said, 'It was horrendous'. A minute or so later I heard screaming from the woman who had gone in before me. It went on and on. Then it was my turn, and yes, it was agonisingly painful, if only for a moment, and, sadly, didn't help at all. A month or so later, I had to have a second injection, which hurt as much, but made no difference either. I had reached the top of the ladder. The only treatment left was spinal surgery: a discectomy and laminectomy, which I resisted for months in the hope it would still get better on its own.

When the two-year mark passed I realised I had to have it. My world had contracted and there was a solution. I was managing because my life had improved and I was working at home, but I was still a bit sad inside as I couldn't go walking and was having to rely on photos of trees taken in the past.

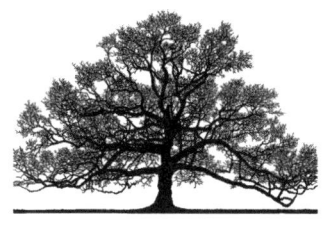

Printing Trees

I was lucky. From finally saying I wanted to go ahead with the operation, to getting it, took just six weeks. When I came round, high on post-op drugs, I immediately got off the bed and stood. It was incredible: there was no pain at all. Standing felt like floating, and it continued to feel like that after the drugs had worn off. Andrew took me home and, knowing he had to be away for work for almost a week, had arranged for a succession of friends and neighbours to come and keep me company and provide me with delicious food. It was delightful. Every day someone new – and no pain.

As I recovered, I gradually started to increase the distance I walked. Just up the road and back to start with, then into the woods and along the river opposite my house. I was eager for new trees and fields to draw and carve, and it would soon be winter, when the tree shapes were properly revealed, so I needed to get out and find them.

Wherever I walk I'm mostly looking at the landscape; the

shapes, the patterns, marks and lines made by a plough or a river, and the trees. I'm also always looking for that special tree, the one I feel a connection with. I take photos of any interesting trees, as sometimes that connection happens later, when I look back over my photos.

I love a wood full of trees, especially when they're oaks with contorted branches, twisting their way up in expressive curves and curls, the ones I often see in exposed upland woods or along the edges of an estuary, where perhaps the wind blasts them into those shapes – or is it just genetic variety? I don't know, but I've found the best of them in an estuary wood on the edge of Plymouth, another in south Pembrokeshire, in various high woods in Wales and in the tiny, old woods on Dartmoor.

I love all the trees for their different qualities. The beeches with their smooth, grey trunks and dainty leaves. The birches with the dark marks on their cream trunks, creating patterns unique as fingerprints, their late winter buds a purple mist in the distance. The hawthorns which blaze white, and occasionally pink, across the moor in spring above the bluebells. The hazels around my house which feed the dormice and squirrels, and the majestic Scots pines which looked back at me every time I glanced up the valley to the edge of the moor, until someone took a chainsaw to them all. Most of all, though, I love oaks, for their variety of shapes, their beautiful trunks and twisting branches, their longevity, and for the huge number of insects they support.

Much as I love trees in woods, my printmaker mind is more attracted to a solitary tree, one in a field or hedge which has had the space to grow, where you can see most of it clearly. I'm not sure why I pick one tree and not another, except that I think I like to have an emotional connection. That might be because of its age, where it is, its shape or just an indefinable quality, an air of having lived a long life and seen much. I think I'm guilty of thinking of large trees as being, in some way, sentient. I thought it was just a sentimental fancy of mine, so was surprised to read about the recent advances in scientific understanding of how trees work, how they can communicate warnings to other trees about insect attacks, how they are linked by fungal networks used to exchange nutrients and information and how a mature tree can support a younger one, effectively feeding it. Of course, this doesn't necessarily give them a consciousness, but until recently even the idea of trees talking to each other would have sounded ridiculous.

People often suggest trees to me. Frequently, they are locally loved trees, ones which everyone knows. I like to go and look at them, but I do find it harder to work with them. Perhaps it's because it feels like they belong to someone else, in the sense that I didn't find them myself, or perhaps because I feel a weight of expectation from everyone, to represent them accurately, or in a certain way. Artists are expected to welcome commissions, where someone asks for a painting or print of a particular scene or tree, but I cannot do them. I've tried, and the whole process just repels me. I've turned down all sorts of opportunities that others would really appreciate. When I'm asked to take on a commission I feel like I should be able to do it, but I know I can't.

I discovered, through trying and failing, that it is vital I have my own connection with the subject matter and develop that through the long process of drawing, carving and printing. Most importantly, I need to feel I'm doing it for me as much as possible, so that I'm pleased with it and it looks and feels right to me, not second-guessing what someone else might think of it. Besides, my process is so long-winded, I always need to produce a relatively large edition of prints to sell so I can make my living. The single trees can take more than a week just to draw on to the plate, then at least a month, and sometimes much longer, to carve. If I just made a single print for somebody, I'd have to charge more than they were prepared to pay, even if I could engage with their subject.

Plenty of artists can talk meaningfully about their work. I've heard sculptors David Nash and Peter Randall-Page talk eloquently and inspiringly. Devon artist Anita Reynolds somehow manages to be both interesting, deeply intellectual and witty when she talks about her beautiful prints and paintings and her deep relationship with landscape.

I've never found it easy, perhaps because I'm primarily concerned with making something, with the craft of it, and then with whether it pleases me visually and prompts an emotional reaction, without really analysing how or why. I don't know if there's anything more than that to my work. If there isn't, I don't mind. I'm always happy to talk about the craft of it, the intricacy of the process, the different methods of registration or how to thicken ink, but those topics are perhaps best left for conversations between printmakers.

My journalism background also makes me allergic to jargon, especially the kind of writing which infects so much of the art world, and which many artists use when talking about their work. Grayson Perry once called it 'International Art English'. It prefers long words and combines them in lengthy and nonsensical sentences. You could be forgiven for assuming it is written with the intention of being impossible to understand, as if that quality alone was enough to elevate the artist's work above the mundane world where people do ordinary things, like go for a walk, or look at a tree, or drink tea from a handmade mug. If mere mortals cannot understand it, then its creator must be a god, and anyone bold enough to point out the emperor is wearing no clothes, by saying

'I don't understand what you're talking about', is simply revealing their own inadequacies.

It's a world where potters become ceramic artists and where the actual craft of making things might even be relegated to assistants, or where an artist is so immersed in an academic environment and the torture it inflicts on language, that they end up writing nonsense. I do realise that most makers who call themselves ceramic artists are simply choosing to make beautiful, but not necessarily usable, objects, and there's nothing wrong with that. However, I think that by using those words they are trying to place themselves higher up a hierarchy of judgement in which there is something utilitarian and thus less valued about being a 'potter'.

I think it might be, at heart, a class thing. The difference between makers and thinkers, those with dirty hands and those in charge. Printmakers, for example, used to be the skilled technicians who would take the artist's vision and reproduce it en masse. They weren't seen as creatives, but skilled craftsmen, artisans, people with a trade. That changed as technology allowed reproductions to be made more easily and the task of most printmakers became printing their own work. But the art world in many ways still tries to distance itself from skills and craft. It is this which makes me a little uncomfortable about identifying with the word 'artist' and all the pretensions and self-aggrandisement that word can carry. Sometimes I do say I am an artist, but more often I say I am a printmaker.

When I lived in south Devon the nearest town was Ashburton, where there seemed to be two sorts of artist or craftsperson. One made mugs and bowls, prints and paintings, and tried to sell them, while the other was centred around more academic artists and craftspeople, many with art school or university connections, whose work tended to the abstract. The two worlds did not seem connected. Both have their place, of course, and I'm not at all against abstract art, but I'm much happier making a living from what I produce, making work which people are more likely to buy and thinking of it as craft.

On a similar theme, there are many sometimes vague, and mostly unspoken, opinions which permeate the world of art and craft making. One is that abstract is better than realist, while another is that a more gestural, 'freer' style is preferable to small, precise mark-making. An engraver creating detailed and gorgeous landscapes by chipping away at tiny blocks of wood risks being less valued than an abstract painter.

When I first started going to the printmaking workshop at Dartington, I sat next to someone who told me she was getting back into art after completing an MA a while ago. In response, I said I had no art training, no art education, couldn't draw and was pretty nervous to be there. She replied kindly, 'But that's wonderful. You'll be so free.' What she meant, I think, was that I wouldn't be burdened with having to learn to draw in a realistic way or by years of being told I should do things in a particular fashion. And I think she was also talking about herself, that she aspired to be 'free', to be able to depict more with less. From where I sat, her carefully drawn and detailed prints were beautiful and skilled. I didn't want to become more 'free': I wanted to be able to depict things like she did.

I honestly think there is room for all, for abstract and gestural, as well as detailed and realistic. I don't think one is better than the other. I love Anita Reynolds' semi-abstract Dartmoor landscapes, as well as those of my friend Val Jones and the beautiful work of Michael Honnor, who taught me printmaking. As Val once said to me when I expressed envy at her ability to produce new work so quickly: 'It's an afternoon of work, but a lifetime of experience.'

The prints made by all three are filled with emotion and drama. They connect me to the landscape and I relate to them through my own memories of being there, or somewhere like it. I also love Hilary Paynter's detailed textural wood engravings, Sarah Gillespie's incredibly intricate charcoal drawings and mezzotints, and I think Thomas Perceval's drawings of trees on the Welsh borders, which he then burns into wood, are very moving.

Many people would probably see my prints as being on the realist/detailed depiction side of art and craft. They're not wrong. When I'm drawing a tree on to my block, I am trying to get my drawing to look like the tree and I'm usually working from a photograph, a practice which is also frowned upon. But, actually, they're not at all realistic in many ways. To start with, they are silhouettes. A normal 2D drawing with light and shade, even in black and white, attempts, at least, with tricks of perspective and shading, to look as if it is 3D, whereas with a silhouette I have little hope of looking anything but 2D.

My trees are also less realistic because they are severely edited. There is no way I can achieve the complexity of an actual tree at the size I print. My trees are more like a cross-section of the middle, a slice of tree. A whole tree usually has a confusion of branches, many of which cross over each other or sit in front of those behind. A realistic silhouette of a tree would end up with big areas of solid black, where the highest number of branches and twigs intersect each other. So far, I haven't wanted mine to look like that. I also edit them in other ways. Sometimes I really like a tree because of something quirky about it, for example a branch which breaks with the general pattern of growth, but often when I draw that tree in silhouette the quirky branch looks ridiculous, so I make it less quirky, or remove it.

The trees which catch my eye are the ones I can imagine

translated into my medium, where there is perhaps less confusion of branches and a strong and pleasing structure.

There is also a question of scale. My trees are not at a large enough scale to allow me to draw the twigs at the ends of branches accurately. If I made them accurate, they would be so small and thin I would not be able to carve around them. So it's a compromise, something tree-shaped but, like every representation, even Sarah Gillespie's and Thomas Perceval's incredible drawings ... and I wish I had their skills ... it isn't the real thing. My depictions are smaller, less dense and much less detailed. But people look at them and see a tree. Some who are local to me even recognise the actual tree I'm working from. And I really do try to put my heart into them, so they somehow reflect back to me the emotions I feel about them, particularly with the choice of background colours and the subtler details.

An art education also seems to make some practising artists feel the need to continually move on, or change. I have a friend who made a series of beautiful images, which sold well, but then her work changed. I asked her why she didn't carry on with the same style and methods, and she said it was important to her to move on. Obviously, developing your skills and challenging yourself has to be a good thing, but for me it depends on how you look at it. I do sometimes feel like a one-trick pony, that I should take more trouble to extend my skills and try new things, and I do occasionally, but I am also happy to thoroughly explore a narrow field. Changes I make to my methods and subject might barely be noticed by someone else, but they are important and experimental to me. I change, but not much. If I compare my early prints with the most recent, they look very different to me, but it has taken me years of small changes to get there.

This isn't without complication, however. I'm mostly happy

doing what I do, but if I wanted to radically change, I might encounter difficulty. Would galleries and private buyers who like my current work be happy with a totally new kind of work? Would people buy it? It is a problem which faces many artists who need to make a living and wish to change. If you're lucky, galleries and buyers can be carried along with you. If not, you might end up having to make bread-and-butter work for sale in galleries while making the new work to please yourself.

A lot of people making art don't sell very much. Many of them, especially if they don't have to make a living out of it, are quite happy with that. But there is also, sometimes, a snobbery here, as if selling your work is somehow degrading it, or you. I've sometimes heard artists tell me rather proudly that they don't sell much. My prints mostly sell quite well and I enjoy selling them. I particularly like doing so at open studios events, where the public is invited to my home or workshop and I get to meet the person buying. I first experienced this at the printmaking workshop, which held an annual sale called Off The Peg, after the way in which prints were pegged to washing lines strung across the room. For years it was wonderfully chaotic, featuring hundreds of prints pegged on both sides of the lines and attended by hordes of potential buyers. Behind the apparent chaos, it was really well run, with printmakers taking payment and packing, others dotted around the room to help the customers, and a system for replacing those sold with others by the same artist. When someone wanted to buy one of my prints for the first time I was thrilled, and that feeling has never worn off.

Over the years I took part in Devon Open Studios many times, inviting people into my home to chat, have a cup of tea and maybe buy something. I also set up stall at many different art and craft shows, starting small, then moving on to larger events.

All the while, I continued walking and looking, taking photos of lines of trees on ridges, majestic spreading oaks in fields and battered hawthorns on the moor, as well as of the patterns in fields made by plough or crop stubble. I thought about printmaking a lot. It was something my mind particularly turned to in quiet moments or when I was walking, trying to think through the stages of transforming an image I liked into a print. It added another wonderful layer to my life and started to change how I looked at the world. Seeing a beautiful view, I felt I was noticing more, seeing the colours differently, noticing the tonal differences and wondering how it could be simplified and translated into an image I might be capable of making.

Printmaking taught me to look more closely. It's a skill I thought I had, but once I started drawing I realised there were many assumptions to overcome. We think we know the shape of things around us, but when asked to draw a familiar object, our minds often intervene and distort our perception of what is in front of us, hence the standard exercise of turning a photograph of that object upside down, then drawing it. It forces the brain to look because the object has been made unfamiliar. I find a similar thing on my different daily walks. The more often I follow the same route, the more accustomed my brain becomes to what it is seeing. It stops looking properly. As I walk my brain ticks off the trees and paths I pass, almost unconsciously, happy that it knows the way. It has no need to notice anything and I have to make an effort to overcome that. When I notice it happening, I sometimes try to trick my mind by walking a route the opposite way round to normal.

One December morning I did just that and the difference was remarkable. I set off into the woods on a day of heavy rain in waterproof coat and trousers. It was morning, but the sky was dark. The wind was from the south-west, mild and wet, blowing up the valley on to my glasses (there are no windscreen wipers for glasses yet, sadly). I paddled down the road and hopped over the gate. Instead of right, I went straight ahead, up a very steep slope I usually prefer to come down. I felt immediately more alert, having to think about the route and whether I had gone too far and missed my turning. The higher I climbed the more misty it became. I could initially see a few hundred feet, then maybe just a hundred. The steepness made me notice what I was walking on, an endless mosaic of leaves, russet brown and grey, oak and beech leaves of different sizes, shapes and tones, every step a unique arrangement. I saw an oak with ferns growing in the moss on its trunk, rather than on the horizontal branches. I must have passed this tree hundreds of times, but had never noticed it was wearing a coat of moss and ferns.

I disturbed a flock of redwings by a group of hollies red with berries. The mist was closing in, turning all the trees, apart from the very closest, into silhouettes of different shades of grey, when suddenly I turned and saw a single beech tree, a sapling maybe 30 feet tall still decked with bright yellow leaves. Around it was a carpet of bracken the colour of rust. The contrast with the grey trees all around was delightful. The misty lack of detail in the trees heightened my sense of their shapes. Everywhere I turned were stunning compositions, trees grouped like ready-made paintings, contorted branches against straight trunks, random lines of trunks like avenues, the closest trees black, the most distant almost as pale as the mist I walked through, which closed in behind me.

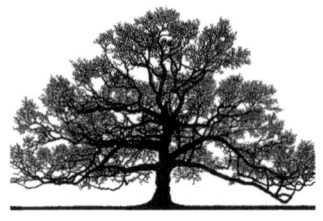

Belonging

Some people belong, and some don't. I've rarely felt I belonged anywhere. Growing up in Wales – where there are degrees of Welshness to which everyone subscribes, even if they don't think they do – I was never very Welsh, although at times I wished I was. I didn't speak the language and didn't have much of an accent. What little accent I had disappeared completely after a few years of living in England. I was alienated by the rugby culture, the narrow 1970s' definitions of male and female and by a toxic family. At university I didn't find many people to fit in with, and in London I forced myself to take part in the gay life on offer, but never felt I belonged. I was most comfortable in Cornwall and Devon, but was still an outsider, often the first gay man people had ever known, and later, in art-related circles, often the only man.

Before I left London to complete the journalism course in Cornwall, I borrowed a friend's car and set off to explore some of Wales, on my own, in the middle of winter. Living in London had somehow made me feel more Welsh and I felt I was missing something, perhaps the familiar landscapes, people and accents I'd grown up with. I'd been reading books about Wales, including Jan Morris' lyrical history-cum-travelogue Wales: Epic Views of a Small Country, which had made me want to explore the country more and, I suppose, see how Welsh I was and whether I might want to move back there. I stayed in B&Bs, plotting a path from east to west, then north to the bottom part of Snowdonia.

I started in Barry, where I was born, staying with my grandmother in her council flat, having a look at the grand but dilapidated high street, the beaches I'd been taken to as a toddler, the views across the sea to the high cliffs of Exmoor and the intriguing islands of Flat Holm and Steep Holm, which guard the Bristol Channel. I remembered going to stay with her as a young teenager, in a flat which seemed half-full of knitting machines. I can still hear my nan's accent and the reedy voices of the old ladies she played whist with. I can picture her working on the gate at Butlin's on Barry Island, sitting in the sun with her 1960s' hairdo and tortoiseshell glasses, looking like the queen of the ticket booth. She used to take me to the funfair for free rides on everything, as she knew the people who ran them, then home for fish and chips or tinned salmon sandwiches and lemon meringue pie. She budgeted carefully, saving money to buy Christmas presents for everyone. She lived a frugal life. She didn't know I was gay, and I didn't tell her.

From Barry I drove to the Gower, where the industrial sprawl of much of south Wales starts to give way to the beauty beyond. I walked the dramatic sweep of Rhossili Bay, with its views to Pembrokeshire, where my parents and their chaos were to be avoided this time. Driving north I entered a less-visited part of Wales, the Green Desert: big moorland hills, lots of sheep and not many people. I stayed at Tregaron, then drove the next day to the ruins of Ystrad Fflur (Strata Florida), a medieval Cistercian abbey and burying place of Welsh princes. Not much has survived, but a magnificent stone arch suggests the wealth and influence of this centre of Welsh culture, where the first history of Wales in Welsh is said to have been written, or perhaps copied out, by the monks, as well as some of the strange and mythic tales of The Mabinogion. I walked from there up a valley between broad hills and across a bare and over-grazed moor. Sheep-ravaged land below, but a red kite above, one of the last survivors, seen only in mid Wales at that time, in the days before much of the UK was repopu-lated with this graceful bird. It was a silent place, with hills and mountains stretching north, east and south as far as I could see.

I left and made my way to Aberystwyth to stay the night with my friend Joyce, then in her late eighties I think. She was an adopter of honorary grandsons, of which she told me I was one. I had met her when I accompanied my mother on a bridge holiday in France, and we had immediately got on really well. She was an amazing woman.

Back in the 1990s, before the internet made such things easier and laws were passed ensuring gay people are protected in the provision of such services, there was a booklet advertised in the gay press listing gay-friendly places to stay across the UK, a mix of genuine B&Bs and small hotels, and a smattering of thankfully obvious places where more than that was on offer. I had nothing against it, but 'permanent house party', as I think the coded language went, wasn't what I was looking for. The only one I wanted to stay in was in a village on the southern side of Cadair Idris, the mountain I had been unable to climb a few years earlier. I drove across the hills to Machynlleth on a day of dark skies, sun and rainbows. I was early, so continued west along the estuary to

Aberdovey, where the elements put on a show: half the sky was a bluish charcoal, the other half orange, turning to red as the sun slid into the sea.

No longer too early, I returned to meet my hosts, a gay couple who had moved from somewhere in England to a Welsh-speaking village, where they ran the post office. This sounded incredible to me, thirty years ago. Not only were they gay, they were also English! I wanted to know what life was like for them. I feared they would be living under siege. They assured me they were really happy there. One of them, if I remember rightly, coached a junior football team, and both of them were learning Welsh. In addition, of course, they had the advantage of running a service vital to a small, rural community. Despite that, I was still astonished. It messed with my preconceptions of being gay in rural Britain, and it made me wonder if perhaps it was possible for me to live in the countryside.

The next day I finally climbed Cadair Idris, on another day of dramatic skies, rainbows, drifting mist and sun. Almost three decades later I can remember the views down the mountain to slopes of bracken lit up rust-red when the clouds parted, west to the sea, east and south to endless hills and mountains. I thought how incredible it must be to live there, to have all that on your doorstep.

I travelled on, taking the mountain road from the village of Dinas Mawddwy, skirting to the south of the spectacular Aran mountain range, through isolated villages then gloriously up towards the second-highest mountain pass in Wales, Bwlch y Groes, where there were more rainbows and deluges. I remember stopping near the top and looking back down to the valley below, glowing bright green as shafts of sunlight broke through the dark clouds.

Much later that day, after driving through mountains and moorland, past Llyn Vrynwy, a reservoir with an eye-catching pumping station, which looks like a gothic castle, and through villages where I wondered what employment there was apart from farming, I arrived in my final destination, Abergavenny. I rose early the next day and climbed Pen-y-fâl (Sugar Loaf), before driving back to London with a familiar sense of dread.

After I finally left London, I returned only once – a quick trip to pick up some stored possessions, my stomach in knots at the prospect of being there. After a decade I returned reluctantly, as a tourist, staying for a few nights in a very nice hotel opposite Canary Wharf, thanks to my friend Kim's air miles. After a magnificent breakfast, Andrew, Kim and I left the hotel to walk along the Thames to the centre. It was a brilliantly sunny day in winter and the tide was in, so the river was broad and blue. There was hardly anyone on the path and those we passed surprised me by saying 'Hello'. The views were spectacular. It felt like a grand European capital city. We walked through miles of former dockland, then from landmark to landmark, past Tower Bridge, The Globe and the Houses of Parliament, before crossing the river. Over a few days, we went to museums, galleries and the theatre. It made me realise that London can be amazing, but that your experience of it very much depends on how much money you have and what state your life is in. Even so, I'm still not sure I could bring myself to spend time in a London gay bar to see if it isn't as awful now as it seemed then ...

I came out to my mother at the age of nineteen, as soon as I returned from university for the first holiday. It was clearly hard for her, because as far as she knew, being gay meant leading an unhappy life and, I later realised, it was too abstract a concept without a boyfriend attached to it. If I had introduced a partner I think it would have been easier. When she eventually met Andrew she immediately liked him, as most people do, and grew to love him.

On occasion she would phone and Andrew would answer. I'd hear him talking and laughing and then, eventually, say, 'Do you want to talk to your son?', to which she presumably replied 'No', as the receiver would go down. Of course, she felt she'd told him all her news and he could pass it on to me. It made me smile. I was so pleased they got on well.

Age nineteen, I was on a roller-coaster of coming out, almost evangelical about it. I told everyone I knew, apart from my father. It took me more than ten years to tell him and when I did, it was in anger. I rarely spoke to him. If he answered the phone, he usually handed it straight over to my mother. However, one day he wanted to talk. He said something I didn't like. I don't remember what. In response I said he didn't know very much about me as he didn't even know I was gay. He went silent, then, genuinely sounding like someone's father, said he had wondered. His reaction seemed quite positive to me – or at least not the resounding negative I would have expected – but sadly, in the following weeks, his ingrained bigotry reasserted itself and he was, according to my mother, quite unpleasant about it all.

I had one other small, but positive, interaction with him, many years later, not long before he died. We visited the house and he met Andrew for the first time. Usually we stayed nearby and met my mother alone. This time we decided to be brave and face him in his house. I was scared of his reaction, so I abandoned poor Andrew and went to help my mother make some tea. I needn't have worried because my father had been brought up to be polite and, on this occasion, he was sober. He was also unwell, suffering from the liver failure which killed him just a few months later. From the hall I heard him say to Andrew, 'Look after him, won't you?' One of just a handful of occasions when I had evidence he cared. I never saw him again.

A year after his funeral service my mother and I set out with his ashes. He had wanted them scattered on the water and the obvious way to achieve that was by asking the pilot boat crew to take us out. Sadly, they told us it wasn't allowed. So we walked to the little pebbly beach where I used to play as a child, and where my brother got into trouble for dangerously diving off a high walkway into water of unknown depth. I perched on a rock and tipped half of his remains into the sea. Later that day we drove to St Ann's Head and scattered the rest just off the coast path, at a spot with a clear view back into the Milford Haven waterway.

I spent a lot of my childhood either trying to get my father's approval or, probably more often, doing the opposite. By the time I researched our family history, he was long dead. It was a shame I hadn't done it earlier, because he would have been interested, I think. The things I uncovered might have connected us briefly, at least.

I discovered his great-grandfather Edward had been a pilot's assistant or 'pilot's boy' in Cardiff in the mid-nineteenth century. I found newspaper stories about him and a colleague rescuing the crew of a French vessel which had been hit by a larger ship, and in a second collision he and another man had to be rescued when their pilot boat was struck by a ship in a blizzard. They were missing for several days until they turned up in Milford Haven, having been picked up by the ship which hit them. I also found out my mother's great-grandfather was a pilot in Cardiff at the same time, so the two men would have known each other.

I started my research after moving to Devon. I thought I'd find out the name Shimell had Jewish origins, which would have been interesting and welcome. I was astonished to trace them back from Wales to eighteenth- and nineteenth-century Teignmouth in Devon, just down the road. I struggled to find baptisms and burials for the Shimells I identified on the censuses, but found reference to a lot of documents listed under the surname at the archives in Exeter. I went to look at them, having no clue what they were. I took a seat and a trolley was wheeled towards me bearing large parchment scrolls. I unrolled one, using the weights I was handed to keep it flat, and did my best to look like I might be able to read and understand it. Suddenly, a lady (who I later learned was the extraordinarily helpful archivist Susan Laithwaite) approached and said, 'I saw your name and what you'd ordered. I've been researching the Shimells for twenty years. They were one of the big Catholic families in Devon.' This explained why I could find no baptisms, because they would have been performed in secret by a Catholic priest, not in an Anglican church.

I traced the family back to two brothers from Shropshire who, unusually, converted to Catholicism in the 1710s. One, also a Richard Shimell, went to Lisbon to train to be a priest and returned under a pseudonym to work for the aristocratic Petre family in Essex, before moving to Chideock in Dorset to be the priest in a 'church' hidden on the upper floor of a barn. My ancestor William, a man with a flamboyant signature and questionable morals, also worked for the Petres as their steward, looking after the administration and rents from their estates in Essex and Devon. He left in disgrace after they discovered he had been using some of those rents to pay off debts he'd amassed. He moved to Devon, where he worked as a lawyer in Totnes, embellishing leases and other legal documents with his amazing signature.

Susan and I travelled to the British Library in London to read letters from, and about, William, and to the Essex archives, where we found an inventory of everything in the rooms occupied by him and his brother at the home of the Petres. The inventory was so detailed you could picture the rooms.

Researching my ancestors made no material difference to my life, but was a revelation which gave me a new connection to Devon and to Wales. I unearthed enough detail to allow my imagination to make characters from the twigs on the branches of my family tree. I often thought about them and the family dramas I had uncovered. I began to experience the strange sensation of having roots and feeling part of something.

Not belonging sounds like a negative experience, and it is in many ways, but it is also a place where it is easier to reinvent yourself. Being on the outside is a creative position, where you can not only see the inside more clearly perhaps than others, but you are also not bound by the ties which sometimes prevent people from changing. What sense of belonging I have comes from love, friendships and the landscape, but also from history.

Shortly after giving birth to me, my mother was diagnosed with diabetes, a condition she struggled with for the rest of her life. After my father died, I thought her life would be easier, and it was in some ways, but I had underestimated how much he somehow managed to look after her, between drinking binges. A year after his death, at the age of seventy-one, my mother was found collapsed, lying on her arm, suffering from diabetic ketoacidosis, a condition brought on by days of high blood sugars, which she had ignored. She had been on the floor for some time. She was taken to hospital, then transferred to the intensive care department at Swansea. As we drove to Wales, I kept in touch with the hospital by phone. My mother's organs began shutting down and she was put on life support. When we arrived at the hospital I was told they could find no pulse in her right arm and almost none in her legs. Her body was grotesquely swollen and she was in an induced coma, surrounded by wires connecting her to machines. They said they would have to amputate her arm, but wanted her to be in a more stable condition before they did so. It was unclear whether her legs could be saved. They said she had a slim chance of survival.

I knew I had to stay there for the duration. I contacted the publications I was working for freelance and found somewhere to sleep. My days became a routine of visiting my mother, talking to her even though she was unconscious, telling her we loved her and she had to get better for Jasper, her dog, talking to the medics and the relatives of the other people in intensive care, and keeping myself sane with small treats of a newspaper, cups of coffee, cakes.

She did lose her arm, but the operation was delayed a little too long and she came very close to death. It took more than two months on the intensive care ward for her to recover enough to move to a general ward, and it was another month in a hospital in Pembrokeshire before she could go home. When she was well enough, I brought Jasper to see her. I had to get permission, find a wheelchair, get her up and out, then bring the dog from the car. If it had been ten times as difficult it would have been worth it, as she came alive when she saw him.

I encountered the very best of the NHS: the extraordinary efficiency, flexibility and kindness of the intensive care staff; and the worst: a ward which was so bad I had to conspire with a doctor to get her transferred to another hospital.

It was the most intensely difficult, emotionally exhausting and completely rewarding time of my life. I'm often filled with doubt, but at that time I knew exactly what I had to do. My mother, on the other hand, thankfully, remembered absolutely nothing about it.

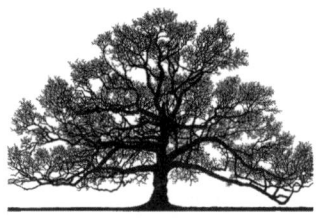

Boro Wood

Probably named after the Saxon word for a fort – 'burh' – as it is topped with a circular Iron Age enclosure, Boro Wood is an ancient woodland, meaning it has been there since at least 1600. The wood is shown on a map from 1604, which was drawn as part of a dispute over land ownership in the area. Its edges, the roads around it and the positions of many of the buildings in the valley below haven't changed since then. For centuries it was a working wood of just under 100 acres, where oak was coppiced for charcoal making, among other uses, with the bark used by leather tanners. This form of woodland management involved cutting patches of trees almost to ground level perhaps every fifteen years or so. The stems were harvested and the stump was left to regrow. This was done rotationally, so every year different parts of the wood were cut back while other parts were regrowing. To make charcoal, which was probably mostly used in the local iron industry, the thick stems were placed in a mound, covered with soil and slowly burned for several days and nights, tended by a charcoal burner.

At some point in the last century the coppicing stopped and the shoots from the centuries-old tree stumps were left to grow, until they became the trunks seen today. The trees are very close together, presumably planted that way to extract the most value from the wood. In more natural woodlands the trees are further apart and do not shade each other out as much. In Boro Wood the density has resulted in most of the trees growing tall and thin as they stretch up for light. When they were coppiced, the stems were cut back before the trees started to shade each other out too much. Now, however, it is dark beneath the trees once the leaves appear and there are few side branches or leaves below the canopy. Although the trunks are mostly quite slim, a closer look at the size of some of the bases gives a sense of the real age of the trees.

The wood was up for sale about twenty years ago and our neighbours Jude Cranmer and husband Mike (who has written a lovely book, The History of Boro Wood) found enough people to put in money to buy it, fearing it might become a conifer plantation. Since then the wood has been managed for nature. The oaks are very slowly being thinned, in the hope that those which remain will spread out more and the extra light will aid a more diverse ground flora. Clearings have been made to provide a variety of habitats and dead wood is being mostly left on the ground. Sadly, it is not open to the public for the usual reasons to do with insurance.

The biggest problem facing the wood is deer. I loved watching the roe deer there, but I came to realise what a threat they were to its future and accept the fact that, in the absence of predators, their numbers needed to be limited. There were no young oaks in the wood because the deer ate all the seedlings, and those trees which were felled did not regenerate from the stump, as they once did, because the deer also ate the regrowth and the tree eventually gave up. When the wood was coppiced, the deer must either have been excluded from the wood by fences, or their numbers kept low. Otherwise the cycle of harvest and regrowth would have been broken. At the top of the wood was a stark illustration of the impact of the deer: a riot of sapling trees inside the safety fence around a nineteenth-century mining shaft. Outside it the saplings were fewer – and none were oak.

Boro Wood doesn't resemble the ancient oak wood of people's imaginations. There are no huge oaks, although along the southwesterly edges there are a few larger ones, which look as if they have been spared the coppice regime, perhaps for the shelter they offer the rest of the wood from the prevailing winds. There are a few signs of rainforest: polypody ferns growing along some mossy branches and even up some trunks, but unlike other woods, in an area which certainly has the right climactic conditions, the trees in Boro Wood are mostly so close together there is a lack of lower horizontal branches for the fern-and-moss-garden-in-the-sky effect we associate with temperate rainforest.

The ground flora is limited mostly to bramble, ivy and bracken, as well as honeysuckle and bilberry, but there are acres of bluebells in spring and some very interesting fungi in autumn. At the northern and eastern edges there's some hazel, and I have found hazelnut shells which appeared to have the distinctive dormouse teethmarks. At the top of the wood are many older beech trees, and the wood is home to, or feeding station for, many birds, including great-spotted woodpecker, ant-eating green woodpecker, nuthatch, treecreeper, goldcrest, firecrest, marsh tit and, in winter, flocks of redwing feasting on the holly berries. Marsh tit, wood warbler, redpoll, siskin, greenfinch and goshawk have also been seen or heard in the woods. I was sometimes scared witless in winter by woodcock, which are impossible to spot until you almost step on them, at which point they erupt into flight, shouting at the tops of their voices. In summer you might see a pied flycatcher, as these have been enticed to nest in bird boxes, put up in the wood as part of a project with the University of Exeter to boost the numbers breeding in the UK. At twilight in the autumn and through winter, the valley is full of the cries of tawny owls. There was a plan to add 270 more nest boxes for a variety of bird species, 10 for large birds, 25 for dormice and 45 bat boxes.

The whole wood is teeming with southern wood ants, so much so that in the summer it is difficult to find an ant-free space to sit down. Their nests are extraordinary in early spring: the tops are dark and glittering with a thick layer of these huge ants in constant motion.

My favourite creatures in the wood are the bats. In a survey in the valley in June 2018 a group of wood shareholders equipped with various detecting devices recorded at least 12 of the 18 species of bats found in the UK, including all three kinds of pipistrelle, barbastelle, brown long-eared, Daubenton's, greater horseshoe, lesser horseshoe, noctule, serotine, whiskered and at least one of the myotis species. A little before dusk in the warmer months, pipistrelle and whiskered bats streamed out from the top of building I lived in, flying like butterflies, some circling and feeding, others heading straight for the trees to feast on insects, including the dozens of oak-reliant species of moths.

A survey of moths in the wood on a single June night in 2002 found 75 species, the list of the common names for which reads like a poem: ghost moth, green oak tortrix, common pug, scorched wing, rivulet, peppered moth, clouded silver, lobster moth, heart and dart, flame shoulder, white ermine, silver Y, small fan-foot.

In summer we occasionally had to rescue a baby bat, whose tiny size makes them vulnerable to becoming exhausted if they suddenly become cold, or it starts to rain, while they are making their first flights. We would find them clinging to the lower parts of our house, put them in a box and take them to a bat specialist who lived nearby. They would be fed live mealworms all day, then brought back and released that evening.

Boro Wood has a special atmosphere due to the make up of its trees, the lack of visitors and the steepness of the terrain. The bottom is at 400 feet above sea level, while the top is a bit less than 800 feet. At just under 100 acres it covers part of one side of a small valley, yet sometimes, before I fully learned the paths, I would get lost in it. If the 100 acres of Boro Wood were open moorland or field you would be able to see the whole space from almost any point within it. There would be little mystery and no slight feeling of hidden danger to keep your senses alert. I love the way woodland creates atmosphere and a sense of the uncanny.

The other side of the valley is also covered in trees. When we moved there a plantation of larches covered the northern end. A walk by the river began with a slightly depressing stroll through the dead zone beneath these trees. Here and there a native tree struggled up through them, but it was not a place you'd choose to linger. Then the fungus Phytophthora ramorum, or sudden oak death, was detected and the larches had to be felled. After the contractors had left, the hillside looked like it had been hit by a hurricane. The work had been done in wet weather and the machinery had gouged great scars across the slopes. They had left huge amounts of brash, and the few remaining native trees looked battered and misshapen. It was good to get rid of the larches, but a shock to see the aftermath.

Over the years I watched the area change. First came gorse and hazel, pushing up through the debris with apparent ease. Within a few years there was birch, ash and rowan, and a few sycamores. Now, perhaps eight or nine years later, the destruction is no longer visible. The area is completely covered with growth and the trees which clung on amid the larches have filled out and flourished. Soon there will be oaks, if the deer don't get them all.

I have walked more often in Boro Wood than any other single place in my life, and yet every walk is different, in subtle ways as one season slowly shifts to another, and dramatically as the weather changes from rain to snow, or sun to mist.

In the autumn there is danger in the wood. As I walked one day in late September there was a sudden breeze, followed immediately by a noise like a distant machine gun, and I was showered with acorns. An acorn falling from a height of 30 feet makes a painful impact with a head. Oaks have mast years in which they produce huge numbers of acorns. These come round every five to ten years. In the valley of the River Ashburn, I noticed this happened in different years on the east and west sides. Along the river on the eastern side, it happened in 2022, when olive-green acorns covered the paths in drifts inches deep, where the rain had swept them down the hill. On the other side, in Boro Wood, I found not a single acorn. I got into the habit of filling my pockets by the riverside and carrying them into the wood. The following year there were so many in Boro Wood they crunched underfoot with almost every step. I gathered handfuls foolish enough to be germinating on the paths and scatter-sowed them wherever the sun hit the woodland floor.

That year I walked in the wood almost every day through the winter. Sometimes I was deep in thought, passing through, getting exercise but not really connecting, while on other days the whole place felt alive and I was part of it. Sometimes I fancifully felt there was no boundary between me and the wood. I wasn't just a human walking through it: I was part of it.

On one showery late November day I set off for my morning walk snug in full waterproofs. The wind was strong, but not cold. I walked my usual route down the road, over the gate into the wood and up a gentle incline parallel to the lane, walking back towards my house, but a little higher up at each step. The sun briefly illuminated the valley floor below, where the little river was full and frothing white in places. The path got steeper and I reached a clearing, where some trees were removed years ago to create a sunny glade, now filling with bracken and self-seeded beeches and the odd rowan. The steepest part of the path lay ahead, as I passed an area of the wood which was thinned perhaps ten years ago. I could see the remaining trees were taking advantage of the extra light, growing new branches lower down the trunks, so the plan was working, at least to some extent. On my left various other north–south rides opened up as I passed.

I was treading on oak leaves, light and dark browns, russet and chocolate, while others, perhaps detached longer from the tree, were black on one side and an iridescent pewter grey on the other. I had never noticed that before, but once I did, I saw these metallic leaves everywhere. Some were small, others enormous. The pattern of colours, shapes and tones on the path was infinitely varied. What was, at first glance, just leaves on a path, expanded in complexity the more I looked.

Stopping and looking closely at what I might have dismissed as just 'moss', I saw there were many different forms of it. The variety is reflected in the lyrical common names for those found in the wood in a survey: common tamarisk, common feather, common smoothcap, swan's-neck thyme-moss, bank haircap, slender mouse-tail.

The wind was increasing as I gained height and the rain was turning from shower to steady. With my hood up, the sound of the wind and the trees resembled the strange ocean roar you get when you press a particular seashell to your ear. My hood was acting like a radar-receiving bowl or the concave shape of a barn owl's face, channelling sound into its hidden ears, amplifying background noises. When I lowered it the quality of the noise and the volume changed instantly.

The path began to level out as I passed an old Devon hedgebank, its construction hidden by a thick coat of moss and ferns. It must once have kept out livestock, or marked a boundary of some kind. I was now walking along the north-western corner of the wood, alongside fields, with a little road visible beyond the gate. Across it, in neighbouring Druid Wood, was a more typically Cornish sight: the remains of a mine engine house. Built to house the equipment for pumping water or the engine powering the cables to lower miners down, engine houses and their distinctive chimneys are dotted all over Cornwall, but I know of only a few in Devon. Parts of this one were not in a good state of repair. Some of the red brickwork from the top of the chimney lay scattered on the ground where gales had tipped it. There is evidence of attempts at mining, probably for tin or copper, in several places in Boro Wood. Along the road at the bottom is a series of adits, horizontal tunnels used for access or drainage of mine shafts, now just dark entrances which have been scaring children for decades. None seems to have been particularly successful in a mining sense. Apart from the deep and frightening shaft next to the engine house in Druid Wood, they all look like little test shafts, prospecting which was soon abandoned. It is also possible local tales are true, that the work was part of an attempt to extract money from investors, who were unaware there was little chance of finding enough copper or tin to make a profit.

The wind was strong at the top of the wood, its volume rising and falling like the sound of waves on the beach, and in what seemed like a similar pattern. First a succession of medium roars and ebbs, then one or two much louder ones, which built up to a crescendo, wind crashing on trees like the seventh wave on shingle. Hood up against the rain, I walked across a pathless stretch, picking my way through long grass and bramble patches around the fallen trunks of gigantic beech trees in various states of decomposition and sprouting fungi, home to communities of creatures nameless to me. I surprised two roe deer, which bounced away, their white rears looking like targets in the falling light. Once they were far enough away to feel safe, they stopped and looked back. They were the largest wild things I was likely to see and such handsome animals. The upright beeches, planted in an avenue to commemorate one of Queen Victoria's Jubilees, presumably in 1887 or 1897, were creaking and groaning in the wind. I thought of the danger of branches falling and paid attention to where the loudest creaks were coming from.

I reached the bank marking the Iron Age enclosure at the top of the wood. It is one of more than twelve hundred scheduled ancient monuments in Dartmoor National Park. It encloses an oval area of many acres. Hut circles have been found inside it. Over the centuries parts of it have been disturbed and probably raided for stone. Natural erosion also must have reduced its height. It is clearly marked on the map of the area from 1604, but the Historic England listing for it expresses uncertainty over whether it was prehistoric or a medieval stock enclosure. It could, of course, be both: an ancient boundary reused later for different purposes.

Inside the circle I stood, breathing and listening, imagining who had walked this space in the past, thinking about ghosts. I continued towards the edge of the wood and stood by a gate, watching the bands of rain crossing the fields and hills, briefly obscuring the triangular beacon of Brent Hill far to the west, where there was another hill fort, that one was two-and-a-half-thousand years old. A beacon fire was perhaps lit there at the time of the Spanish Armada. Below me I could see part of the little town of Ashburton, snug between two hills, stretching south on either side of the river. The sun broke through, making the rain glow silver just before a violent squall of wind and wet made me retreat into the holly, like a woodland creature. The sound of rain and wind on the trees was loud, but short-lived.

A little further down the wood I reached a clearing with a magnificent view west, across Hembury Woods and the tree-filled basin of the River Dart to the high moors more than five miles away.

When the printmaking workshop at Dartington decided to stage an exhibition of handmade books, I decided to make one filled with images of oak trees and moths, with a feel, hopefully, of what I found so entrancing about Boro Wood.

I looked at the group's previous books. They all had prints on one side of the paper only. As you turned the pages every other one was blank. I decided I didn't like that much white space – I wanted images on both sides. I came to regret that decision. It was a very risky approach, as it meant I would be printing images on the back of other images. Obviously, if one went wrong, I would not only be spoiling that print, but the one on the back as well.

The process of planning the book was mind-boggling, and it took many weeks to complete the printing. But it was such a creative and rewarding project, even though I only made three of the eight I'd planned, and I only sold one of them.

I made dozens of moth shapes from thin plastic and stumbled

on a way of visually showing the intrinsic link between moths and the oaks they relied on, by printing the moth shapes with the pattern of oak branches. I spent a long time experimenting with gold inks to make a luminous background on which to print a tree. I also learned how to use gold leaf in an attempt to show the iridescent dust I imagined falling from moth wings as they ascended into the night sky. I did this by using a toothbrush to flick tiny dots of glue, then pressing a sheet of gold leaf on top, brushing away the excess to leave a glittering cloud of moth wing scales.

My book joined dozens of others in an exhibition at MAKE Southwest in Bovey Tracey, Devon. Some of those taking part were worried the books might be damaged by visitors turning the pages, so all sorts of precautions were taken, including having two printmakers present at all times. However, on the days I stewarded the exhibition, the opposite was true. The biggest risk was that no one would see anything, because the public were so considerate they didn't dare touch the books. We removed the plastic sheets covering them and opened them all, but even so we had to tell each visitor they were allowed to touch them and turn the pages.

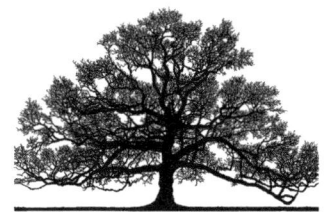

Snow and Fog

What I love about snow and fog is how they change the familiar into something new and wondrous. Falling snow hypnotises me. I cannot take my eyes away from the steady transformation of the view. I watch as it softens and brightens, covering up the unsightly and unifying the landscape. Objects start to disappear, their outlines visible for a while, then blurring and merging with others.

Fog also softens and hides. It turns the ordinary into a mystery, removing colour and detail, transforming objects into entrancing silhouettes in tones of grey. It plays with distance and scale, making it hard to be sure whether that upright figure is a person or a tree.

It's rare that snow falls in daylight hours in southern Britain, but if it does, I want to cancel whatever I have planned so I can sit and watch it. When it is forecast to fall in the night, I have even been known to make sure I wake in the early hours, turn on an outside light and watch, shivering in a dressing gown, entranced by the dancing flakes.

When I was a child in west Wales, living down a long lane half a mile from a small village, there were two very severe winters, the worst of which saw massive amounts of snow. It fell for more than twelve hours in strengthening winds. I was fascinated by the way the house created a barrier to the wind, swirling the snow to make almost circular drifts on the drive. Overnight much more fell, driven by strong winds into enormous drifts, leaving some rural areas cut off for weeks. Snow banked up against some houses to such a depth people couldn't open the doors and had to climb out of the upstairs windows. In parts of Pembrokeshire food and medical supplies had to be delivered by helicopter or boat.

From an early age it was my job to wake up my parents with a pot of tea on a tray, so one of them could drive me to school, about five miles away. I'd then go downstairs and make my breakfast, listening to Radio 1 and reading at the same time. Certain tracks from the 1970s are forever bonded in my mind with particular books and the emotions evoked by them.

During this strange role reversal I also had to make sure they hadn't dozed off again, so I would wait ten minutes then go back upstairs to check. When I reached the age at which I could drive a moped, they were very happy to get me one, as it meant they no longer had to drive me to school (although the morning tea tray routine continued long after). I was also delighted to have more independence, and relieved I would no longer have to wait for my father to pick me up, not knowing what state he would be in. Sometimes I would see his car coming up the hill towards the school and could tell he had been drinking. When he was really drunk, the drive home was a scary experience, as the car weaved all over the road. Part of me was scared we were going to crash, but mostly I was just embarrassed. I fantasised about demanding he stop and let me out, but where would I have gone?

Snow and Fog

The morning after the blizzard I got dressed and went straight out to see how much snow had fallen. I had never seen so much. In the garden there were drifts 4 or 5 feet high, but the scale of it didn't become apparent until I managed to scramble part-way up the lane. I saw drifts at least 10 feet tall, perhaps 15 feet in places, the snow having been pushed through the hedge to completely fill the lane in shapes like giant breaking waves. The landscape I knew so well had turned black and white as far as I could see. The winter trees were stark and stunning against the white fields and grey sky. The world was transformed. I'd never seen anything so amazing.

I didn't manage to convince my parents about the depth of snow and the enormity of the task, as they sighed and told me we'd just have to get shovelling. When they finally got out, they realised it wasn't going to be possible. We were cut off until the snow melted. With the whole county buried, there was no chance a snowplough would come down our little lane, nor would a tractor have been able to get near enough to clear it.

The blizzard had also knocked out our electricity supply. We had no power for more than a week. My father attempted to walk a few miles to a village near the sea, where a pilot boat could have picked him up and taken him to work, but he soon gave up.

The temperatures remained below zero for several days after the blizzard, then it warmed slightly and rained before freezing again. Rather than melting the snow, however, the rain froze instantly to everything it touched, including the power lines, many of which came crashing down. Households which hadn't lost power in the blizzard now found themselves without it. The rain also froze on the drifts into a layer of ice thick enough to bear my weight. Now I could walk on top of the snow, which was so deep I was level with the telephone wires.

The temperature plummeted and it snowed again. It was colder than I'd ever felt before. But the sky also cleared and the sun came out. From my vantage point on top of a 10-foot drift in the lane, I could see the landscape glittering into the distance, as every twig and branch was wrapped in ice, sparkling in the sun. At sunset the colours of the sky twinkled in the ice, and the shadows in the holes left by my footprints in the snow were an otherworldly deep blue.

The attractions of staying in the house soon paled, and I decided to walk the three miles or so to see my friend Sarah, who later became my girlfriend. Once I got on to the larger roads, it was surprising how easy it was to walk, as the drifts didn't extend all the way across, and where there were no drifts, the snow was not deep. It was strange to see how the wind had driven all the snow into a mound many feet high, while right next to it there was virtually no snow at all.

In places I had to squeeze between the end of a drift and the hedge, but earlier walkers had managed to cut paths through the edges of the worst of them. It was like being in a Brueghel painting. There were quite a few people on foot, bundled up in layers of clothes, some with scarfs wrapped around their heads and hats. By then, some people were running out of food. The village shop had not been supplied since the blizzard, so they were walking to the next nearest place, about three miles away. After several days cooped up with my parents, it was wonderful to see Sarah.

For me, at first, the loss of electricity was part of the excitement of everything being different. We had oil central heating (but it didn't work without electricity) and an electric hob and oven, so my father placed two enormous logs in the hearth of the open fire, leaving a gap between them in which a fire could be lit. A metal grid across the top of the logs allowed saucepans to be placed above the flames, so food could be cooked. When the logs burned through and the grid couldn't be supported, we added new logs. The biggest problem was lack of hot water for baths or showers. Washing had to be done either in cold water or a small basin of warm.

A few days later I walked the longer distance to Milford to see friends and buy anything I could find on a list my mother gave me. She had already walked to the nearest dairy farm to get milk, and luckily, she always had a well-stocked freezer, but we had no bread, and candles were running out.

When the snow eventually started to melt we were astonished to discover that under a drift on the road at the end of our lane was a car, abandoned in the blizzard, buried for almost two weeks. I had walked over it many times, not even knowing it was there. No snowplough or tractor ever came down the lane. It was more than two weeks before it was clear enough for a car.

Years later, I discovered the magic of freezing fog, while on holiday in the Quantock Hills in Somerset one Christmas with my friend Trish, with whom I had shared houses in Brighton, then London. At the bottom of the hill, where we had rented a house, the fog was dense and had rimed the trees with a thick layer of frost. We decided to walk up the hill to get to the ridge-top path. As we brushed against the bushes there were little explosions of frost particles and the occasional gentle breeze showered us with white crystals from the trees above. As we climbed we wondered if it was a good idea to be exploring in conditions so conducive to losing your way.

We plodded on, up and up ... then all of a sudden we were in sunshine, looking down on a layer of solid cloud, as if in a plane. It reminded me of a scene in the 1970s' remake of the film Lost Horizon, where a group of westerners in the Himalayas are led through ice and snow to a balmy hidden valley called Shangri-La. If I remember rightly, they enter a cave, then get their first astonishing glimpse of the valley below, where it is sunny and warm, and the inhabitants live unfeasibly long lives. Our Shangri-La was far from warm, and was up, not down, but there was no fog and it certainly felt like we were in another world. The conditions remained the same for the whole of our walk along the ridge and back: blue sky, sunshine and penetrating cold, as if we really were walking where planes fly. As we reached the lip of the hill and started to descend the steep path, we experienced the reverse: we had to walk back into the fog. It was an act of faith in the continuation of a path we couldn't see. It was like plummeting into nothingness. Our feet remained on the ground, but it felt like falling.

When I was living in south Devon I was lucky enough to experience another period of freezing fog. 'Lucky' because fog itself doesn't happen that often, and freezing fog is a rare opportunity to see the world transformed in a particular way. I know it's not everyone's cup of tea, and it can be a nightmare for drivers, but I love it in the same way I love snow and the waking up of the countryside in spring. Such changes refresh our view of the world. When the landscape returns to normal after a few days of lying snow or a day of freezing fog, for a while it is also something new. I look at it more closely and notice things I would not have seen otherwise.

On this occasion the weather had been very cold for some days, followed by thick fog on the moor. The next day the fog thinned and we went for a walk around Buckland Beacon with our friends Olwen and Nicholas. A group of beech trees was so completely covered in thick, white rime, it looked like someone had sprayed it with icing. Everything had been bombarded with millions of tiny, super-cooled water droplets, which froze the instant they touched a solid object. Every blade of grass was double its size, enlarged with an outline of ice, and the little ponds were frozen over. Most beautiful of all to me, though, was the rime on the granite rocks of the tors. A gentle breeze must have caused the fog to eddy and swirl between the rocks and their crevices, causing it to lay down lines of white mist-frost like the circular maze patterns of Celtic designs.

Walking in dense fog is a bit like walking in the dark. All the familiar direction markers are gone until you're a few feet away from them. It makes us look really closely at everything around, as our brain goes into overdrive trying to work out where we are. Of course, there are no views, and on the moor that can make it a bit boring, but I can't help thinking this experience of basic human vulnerability is good for us occasionally, in that it stimulates a part of our brain which becomes complacent when all it sees is familiar. I also think that the temporary loss of something, even of a view, helps us value and appreciate its return. I have walked on Dartmoor a few times in thick fog, sometimes intentionally, sometimes caught high up as the cloud descended and the path disappeared. I've never got lost in it, perhaps only because I was usually following paths I knew.

Extreme cold is also rare in southern Britain, but in January 2010, when I was living in Lapford, in the middle of Devon, there was a record-breaking winter. I had been living in the south-west of England for almost fifteen years by that point and the climate had been mild. In Cornwall, even on the higher ground where I made a garden in front of the terraced house I had bought, it was unusual to have frost, let alone snow. I filled the garden with exotic and tender plants and hardly lost any.

By the time we moved to our first house in Devon I had become more interested in gardening and, with Andrew's help, made one out of a weedy 180-foot-long space. When we arrived it was a mess, mostly overgrown lawn, which was riddled with invasive couch grass. There weren't any steps down to it, just a muddy slope to negotiate, at the bottom of which was what had been described to us as an 'unfinished patio': a pile of rubble and gravel, dumped there when the previous owners dug out the drive, ordered too much gravel for it and didn't know where else to put it.

I gradually made borders and filled them with grasses and perennials. I decided to use the rubbly area to my advantage. I smoothed over the rubble pile, added soil and turned it into an area for dry-loving plants, many on the tender side. We dug up the lawn and paving stones at the top and made a gravel garden with more grasses, perennials, exotics and small trees. For years the mild winters continued and the garden flourished. I even contacted the National Garden Scheme (NGS) to see if they'd have me. The rather posh man on the other end of the phone asked me how large my garden was. I told him about 180 feet long. 'Not very large, then,' was his reply. Of course, many of the gardens raising money for charity by opening their gates to the public are enormous country-manor-types, so perhaps that was his perspective. As far as I was concerned, it was the largest garden I had ever had.

A much more friendly lady was sent round to view it. She thought it was good enough, so we did open it to the public in the end, and were even featured on a television programme about new NGS gardens, which meant I was visited by the delightful Carol Klein and a camera crew. I already knew I had been accepted into the scheme, but the television people wanted what they would call 'jeopardy': would something work, or would it be a disaster? They wanted the programme to hinge on whether the garden was accepted into the scheme or not, and all the work I had to do to make it good enough, so I had to go through the whole application process again for the camera. The friendly NGS lady made a second visit, though this time she was coached to be much more critical. It was all very silly: her finding things to criticise and having to repeat her comments multiple times as every shot had to be done from different camera positions. I found myself becoming quite annoyed at her, even though I knew it was all staged.

Eventually, towards the end of the 2000s, the decade or so of mild winters ended and a succession of cold and snowy ones started, turning the tender plants in the garden into sludge overnight. We had left the heating on as it was forecast to be unusually cold. By the morning the thermometer in our sheltered porch was showing minus 12°C. I decided to walk to the village shop. I wasn't wearing a hat, and after a few minutes my head started to hurt. I didn't immediately associate it with the cold, but soon realised I wasn't developing a headache: it was just colder than I had ever felt in the UK. Car temperature sensors registered minus 19°C early that morning and the record-breaking cold continued for days. Rather than compressing and hardening into a crusty layer, the snow on the ground stayed strangely light and fluffy for more than a week, as if it had just fallen.

Walking on Dartmoor with Andrew on a sunny day while the snow was still thick on the ground, I was unnerved to see a bank of bright, white cloud sitting part-way down a ridge, gently sliding towards us. The sky was a deep blue and there were no clouds in it, but here was one on the ground. It looked like the leading edge of a sandstorm, beautiful but ominous.

The longest period of bitter cold I have ever experienced came when I spent a year in France as part of my degree. I stayed in Lyon, which doesn't have a reputation for being particularly cold, but that January there was a lot of snow and it was bitterly cold for weeks, with some days not getting above minus 10°C and night-time temperatures which were even lower. I was living in student halls, which were wonderfully warm, and the radiator in my room was permanently hot. Despite that, moisture condensed and froze on the window just above it. The thick layer of ice partly defrosted in the day, dripping down the glass, then froze solid again at night. Outside, it was so cold my first few breaths made me cough. Water pipes to houses and flats all over the city froze and burst, then thawed in a brief warm period before the cold returned, freezing the dripping water into cascading ice sculptures completely covering the fronts of some buildings. Coming home in the early hours after a night out with friends, walking through a deserted and snowy city, we heard a strange creaking noise as we approached the pedestrian bridge across the river near the Palais de Justice. As we looked down we saw the water was full of ice floes, grating against each other as the current pulled them on towards the Mediterranean.

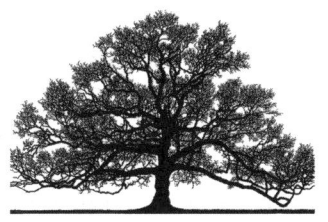

Almost Wales

We decided to move from Devon simply because we wanted new places to see and new landscapes to walk in. At times it seemed like a strange decision, as we loved living there and had lots of friends and connections, but sometimes a change and a new start is needed. It was still a wrench to leave, though. Every time I saw friends, I wondered when I would see them next. Every time I walked in Boro Wood for weeks beforehand, I felt like I was saying goodbye.

Dawn flooded the valley with an amber light on the day of my last walk. The sky was cloudy, but there was colour everywhere; the clouds glowed and the light on the woods made all the browns golden. I felt quite teary after an emotional week of goodbyes, including a little party to thank Andrew for all the voluntary work he had done for several community groups in recent years. As I walked along the familiar paths I heard a buzzard's distinctive 'pee-uuu' cry and remembered how, during my time in London, I had longed to live somewhere I could see these magnificent birds from the house. In later life, it was always a confirmation I was in the right place. I looked up and saw two circling the valley. I watched them for a while until they passed from view. A bramble caught the lace of my boot and I nearly fell, as if the wood was trying to keep hold of me. I walked to the top and looked out at the other woods in the distance. I skirted the southern edge, suddenly blasted by wind. I passed the bluebells, asleep, or maybe just waking, beneath the leaf litter. I walked with sadness back to a house which was soon to be someone else's home. It was the house where I had discovered printmaking and where I had experienced the most prolonged period of happiness in my life. It was a match for the houses I had viewed with envy while walking in the country on trips away from London.

We had been coming to the area around Hay-on-Wye for years. We really liked Hay, which is similar to Ashburton, but a little smaller, with bookshops instead of antiques and bric-à-brac shops. It also had galleries, good cafés, a fantastic bakery and an eclectic mix of people. The landscape around it is stunning. Above are the Black Mountains, the westernmost upland of the Bannau Brycheiniog (formerly Brecon Beacons) National Park. Below is the River Wye, beautiful but suffering a slow death due to pollution from farming run-off, especially from the number of nearby chicken farms. Across a stream on the eastern edge of Hay is England, rural Herefordshire with its sticky red soil, orchards draped with mistletoe and, almost everywhere you look, huge old oak trees. On the eastern side of the Black Mountains is Golden Valley, which has an extraordinary number of public footpaths and is one of the few areas of England which had native Welsh speakers in relatively recent history. Maps of the area, and of much of the English side of the Herefordshire border lands, are full of

Welsh names for farms and geographical features. My American friend Emily perceptively asked if I was still moving to what she had christened 'Almost Wales'.

Around Hay the many Welsh names for streets and places have become anglicised. I haven't heard anyone use their Welsh pronunciation. Heol y Dwr (Water Road) has become something that sounded like 'oily door'. I realised there was no point pedantically pronouncing it in a Welsh way as I might not be understood, but couldn't bring myself to say 'oily door' either. Both sides of the border are neither entirely English, nor entirely Welsh. A bit like me.

We were buying a house in Golden Valley, but, for many reasons, we had to pull out. With just a couple of days to find somewhere to live before exchanging on our house in Devon, we were lucky to find a converted barn to rent, about four miles from Hay. It had been for sale, and we had previously viewed it, but had decided it wasn't for us because of its proximity to a busy road. The house was the most modern, and the poshest, I had ever lived in, with bifold doors opening to beautiful views over farmland to Hergest Ridge in the far distance. In the middle of the view was the valley of the River Wye, which was often filled with a band of mist on winter mornings. To the east were the wooded slopes of Merbach Hill and south was an upland common called Little Mountain.

I didn't walk for days after moving in. I was busy sorting out the house, but was also disconcerted. In order to reach a footpath without getting in the car, I first had to brave walking on the busy road. There was no pavement or walkable verge. There was a 40 mph limit, but most cars went faster. It felt dangerous. In Devon I had walked along our single-track lane every morning. Even then I used to get annoyed at the speed of some drivers, until I tried an approach some might view as high risk. Rather than flattening myself into the hedge so they could roar past as if I wasn't there, I walked a couple of feet out into the road. There was still enough room for them to pass, but they instinctively slowed down. I also pretended I didn't know they were there until they were fairly close behind me. Then I would stop, turn, look towards them and step back a foot. This prompted them to lift their hand in thanks. I would wave back. Everyone smiled. But here, with cars hurtling along at 50 mph+, that strategy was much too dangerous.

I felt quite disconnected from my surroundings and a little lost without my familiar walks. I enjoyed the view from the house, but it felt a little like watching something on television. I wanted to be in it. I was excited to be somewhere different with new places to walk. I bought maps and stared at them, looking for routes I could take nearby, but talked myself out of following any of them. In the end, I forced myself to walk on the road the few minutes it took to reach the lane up the hill to Little Mountain. I even moved on to the verge for the cars coming towards me, waved and got a wave back. Once I was on the little side road there were no more cars.

There had been hard frosts for several nights in a row and sections of the road up the hill were covered in a thick layer of ice, where water draining from the fields flanking it had frozen. I walked carefully. I passed through a farm, setting off barking alarm dogs on both sides. I looked back and saw the big fields on the floodplain of the River Wye and beyond it the hills. There were glimpses of river, reflected white in the sun. I reached the edge of the common, passed through a gate and headed up a steep track, deep with mud, which was thankfully frozen. There was mistletoe everywhere, a bright greeny-yellow, chartreuse perhaps, a word which conjures up the contents of a 1970s' drinks cabinet ... advocaat, Blue Nun, cherry brandy. The quantity of mistletoe and the number of large oaks are the two things I most notice about the west Herefordshire/east Powys countryside. Some smaller trees are so covered with mistletoe you can barely distinguish a trunk or branches. Tall slender trees on distant field margins are dotted with round shapes, as if decorated with giant, raggedy balloons. The oaks are everywhere, much larger and more frequent than in Devon. Have they grown larger because the soil is better? Or have they just escaped being felled for reasons not known? Huge, stately oaks on field edges are ten a penny, while even older, veteran oaks with enormous, but hollowing trunks are frequently seen. At the top of the frozen path was the common, dotted with hawthorns, some with trunks like oaks, thick and scaly, gnarled with age. Most of it was close-cropped grass and bracken, with seedling foxgloves by the thousand. Here and there were a few rowan saplings, and around the edges the woods were advancing. I could see the high points of Hay Bluff and Twmpa to the west, looking like upturned ship hulls jutting out into the landscape. I was interested to know the altitude, so looked it up on an app, which showed the summit on which I was standing to be 995 feet, so even when 1,000 feet was considered the height above which a hill became a mountain, Little Mountain wouldn't have qualified. I thought of the film The Englishman Who Went up a Hill but Came Down a Mountain, in which a Welsh community is determined to foil English cartographers and add enough height to their hill to make it a 1,000-foot mountain. I decided I must be The Welshman Who Went up a Mountain but Came Down a Hill.

I like to walk in the morning, waking up as I move, thinking about the day ahead and getting a bit of exercise. Little Mountain is too long a walk for that, but one day my new neighbour Gill drove me a mile up the road to see some interesting trees near a church. I connected the walk we did with another footpath and decided that would be my default morning walk. On the map it looked like nothing very much: a church, a few fields, a small wood. But, like so many walks, it got more interesting on closer examination.

Starting at a church enclosed by a handsome wall and some large yews, I walked across a field passing two large oaks, one seemingly pollarded, with an array of branches radiating out from a point maybe 10 feet up the main trunk, in a lollipop shape. It reminded me of a tree on which I based the print Dartmoor Oak. I crossed another field just as a ray of sun lit up an impressive oak a few fields away, as if saying 'Draw me!'. Mist hung in the woods on Merbach Hill and over the distant river. In front of me was an attractive clump of oaks stranded in the middle of a field on the edge of a wood. On the other side of the field, the sun was just coming up over Little Mountain, silhouetting a hedgeline of trees, whose shadows fell on emerald grass around me.

I passed through a gate and walked down to a stream. It looked like a winterbourne, probably drying up in summer, though as I crossed a little bridge I noticed the fence between me and the stream was lined with leaves to quite a flood height, so it clearly had potential to turn into a torrent after heavy rain. The path was slippery with Herefordshire mud, a deep reddish-brown with few stones to bind it together and give grip to my feet. It felt like walking on lard. There were large, old oaks in the wood beyond, behind a fence. The path continued through a transitional zone between wood and fields. It looked like it had once been pasture, but now there were hazels dripping yellow catkins, birches, hawthorns and ash, and evidence of cow parsley, dock, bracken and bramble: those first colonisers of land left to its own devices. There were also a few young oaks, so somebody must have been keeping the deer population in check.

On the map the wood looked tiny, just a sliver of trees surrounded by large fields, but this wilded edge made it larger. I wondered if it had been saved from the plough, or the cow, because it was in a dip on wetter land. My bird app noted the songs of the usual suspects: robin, wren, blue tit, jay, song thrush, chaffinch and crow, but also blackcap, siskin, marsh tit, firecrest, coal tit and redwing. I was so pleased to hear the redwing, a link to Boro Wood. To my delight, I also heard the crazy laugh of a green woodpecker and the drilling of what was probably its greater spotted cousin.

There was more evidence I was walking in what had been a field not so long ago: a moss-covered stile, no longer needed as there was now no fence or hedge, and a drinking trough for livestock, clogged up to the top with years of fallen leaves. The low sun made the branches yellow. There was frost on the leaves on the path here still, but it hadn't been cold enough to freeze the ground. This insignificant slip of green on a map, becoming richer and more diverse, could be swept away so easily, I thought. I spotted some large drainage tubes lying on the ground and offered up a silent prayer that its transformation into woodland be allowed to continue.

A few weeks into our time in this converted barn, while setting up my press with difficulty (I had lost some of the nuts and bolts in the move), I took a break and happened to look out the back about half an hour before dark. The sky was colouring up for sunset and the light was golden. I sensed a movement in the field beyond the garden hedge and saw a large, pale bird land on a post. I've seen barn owls before, but not often, and then only a glimpse in the dark, usually from a car. This one flew over the field, low and hovering, moth-like, flying here and there for half an hour. It honoured us with its presence at the same time for several days, but I've not seen it since.

A week or so later, I was watching the fields at a similar time and saw a bird of prey land in a tree some distance away. It soon took off again and circled the fields below the house. It was flying low and, as it turned, I saw its forked tail and noted its languid wingbeats, as if its wings were slightly hinged in the middle, as well as where they joined its body. As it rotated its underside towards the sun, I caught my breath as the cream, grey and rust of the belly of this red kite were transformed by the golden light into brilliant yellows and reds. It gently wheeled above the garden, forming overlapping circles, then drifted slowly away.

We had spent weeks touring the area, getting to know the villages and landscapes, with an eye on where we might like to live, and where we wouldn't. Everywhere we went I saw beautiful, big oaks, sometimes shouting 'Stop!' at Andrew, so I could jump out of the car and take a photo.

On a walk by the River Wye at Bredwardine, Gill showed me five or six veteran oaks, a few clearly in their last decades. I went back on my own a month or so later, when the path was lined with blackthorn blossom and the snowdrops were long gone. I passed the old yew in front of the church, which would take the outstretched arms of a small family to encircle. I opened the gate and set off down the river path, which was inches deep in glutinous mud. I looked up and saw a veteran oak with a trunk so fissured it reminded me of the ventral grooves on a whale's throat. It had lost many of its limbs and was in the process of losing another. One branch was almost entirely shorn of bark, yet still showed buds on the twigs at the end: battered, part-broken, but still alive. The next was the largest, not in height, but in girth, with branches spiralling out from a central belly like tentacles.

Then another two oaks and two old ashes and, finally, the smallest, but possibly the oldest of them all: an oak at the end of its life. It was little more than a stump with two branches, standing alone in a field, slowly melting into the ground.

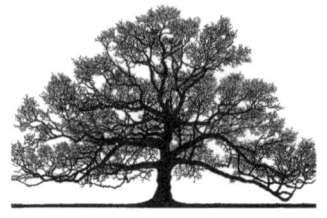

Acknowledgements

Thank you to Cath Burke from Little, Brown for messaging me on Instagram, wondering if I'd like to talk about a book. I thought it might be a scam, but it turned out to be real. Thank you to everyone at Little, Brown who has helped make this happen.

Thanks to Andrew for doing almost everything else so I could concentrate on writing, and to my friends for being interested and encouraging me.

Thank you to everyone at the Dartington Print Workshop and to those who have bought my work over the years.

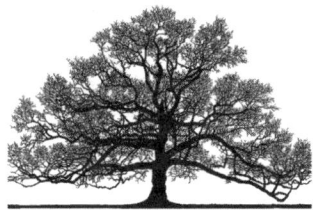

About the Author

Richard Shimell was born in Wales. He switched careers in his forties from journalism to printmaking, following a conversation over the garden fence. He loves working for himself so much he is now happily unemployable. He walks in all weathers.

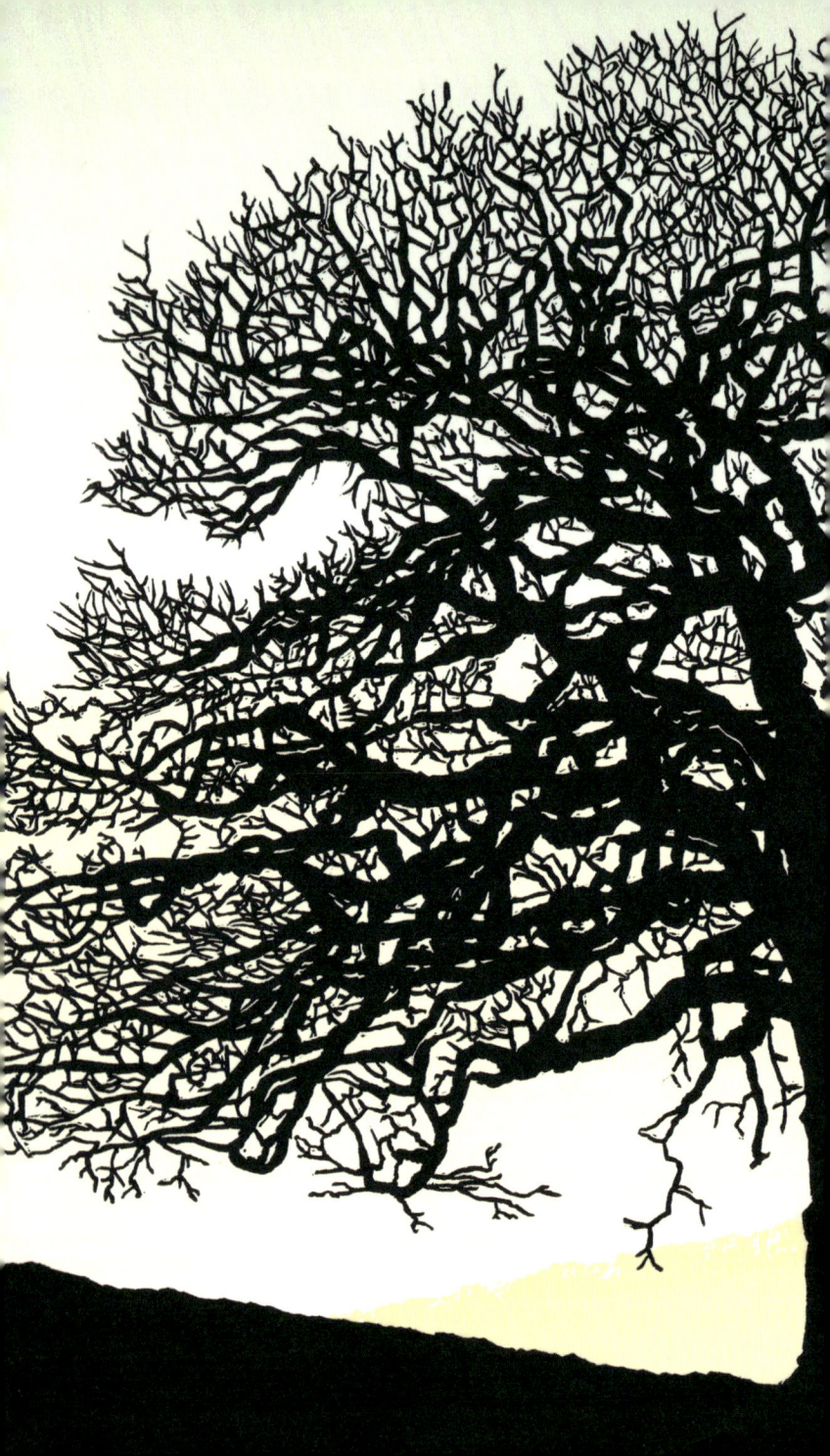